GET BACK UP Again

Discover the power
to get back up again

Dr. Teco Manuel

GET BACK UP

Discover the power
to get back up again

Again

Dr. Teco Manuel

T&J PUBLISHERS

A SMALL INDEPENDENT PUBLISHER WITH A BIG VOICE

Printed in the United States of America by
T&J Publishers (Atlanta, GA.)
www.TandJPublishers.com

All Bible verses used are from the King James Bible (KJV), the New King James Bible (NKJV), New Living Translation (NLT), and the New American Standard Bible (NASB)

Cover design by Timothy Flemming, Jr. (T&J Publishers)
Book format and layout by Timothy Flemming, Jr. (T&J Publishers)

ISBN: 978-0-9994121-9-0

To contact author, go to:

DrTecoManuel@gmail.com
Facebook: Teco Lamones Manuel
Twitter: Teco Lamones Manuel
Instagram: Teco Lamones Manuel

ACKNOWLEDGMENTS

Wow, what can I say, this project has taken almost seven years, involves some of the most horrific struggles of my life, and demonstrates how much I owe to Jesus, for providing these principles to assist those experiencing the ebbs and flows in life.

Unfortunately, if Christians don't understand that every moment of their lives is not going to be a ray of sunshine, many will walk away from the faith when challenges arise. For this reason, God commissioned me to chronical the highs and lows of my life to show His master plan to prosper us.

Favored of the Lord, I am blessed to be a witness that with God, all things are possible, and know from experience that you can get back up again. I am grateful for the love of my life, Tiffiny, who not only enjoys the favor of God with me but she has also endured every struggle right by my side as a Helpmeet and soldier of Jesus Christ. To my son Tyler, I love you man, and I declare as God did to the world, "you are my beloved son whom I am well pleased." Then to my parents, thank you for giving me life and for supporting Tiffiny and me as we transitioned from military life to ministry. I love you Mother, Dad, Pop, Mama J., Momma, and my Godmother, Mama Net. I would also like to bless my Godchildren, Vernessa and Malachi; I love both of you, and I thank God for you. Lastly, I would like to thank those who carry the Bloodstained banner and all of my Wounded Warriors around the world for supporting Tiffiny and me; I love you.

Now let us get back up again!

TESTIMONIAL

"The primary challenge facing believers today is that of proper management of everyday life challenges. In this book, Bishop Teco Manuel masterfully reveals a robust and proven method of facing discouragement, adjusting to daily life and how to control the feelings one gets when one becomes overwhelmed.

Using everyday principles derived from sports and other activities, Dr. Manuel provides an uplifting and life-altering process to face everyday life and overcome the trials that everyone encounters at one point or another in their life. He also makes it abundantly clear that believers also experience struggles. Unfortunately, modern Christendom has believers face their challenges with a pie in the sky mentality, thus forcing the believer to create and cause conflict in their walk of faith.

I highly recommend this book to anyone who is facing life and its struggles. As a leader of leaders, I also recommend this insightful guide to individuals who minister to ordinary folk every day and watch them struggle with the challenges of life but have a desire to see them become overcomers."

+Darel E. Chase, Ph.D.

TABLE OF CONTENTS

FOREWORD

Resiliency is one of the signature character traits of a true believer. The innate ability to withstand attacks, difficult setbacks, and in some cases, endure suffering and still possess the adeptness and dexterity to rebound with an even greater inspiration to move forward has to be celebrated for what it really is; the power of God working within.

In this insightful literary gem, Teco Manuel expounds masterfully on "Bouncing Back" from the many challenges of life, particularly for Christians. He rescues us from the towers of failure, fear, and flaws as well as from the menacing dragons of depression, despair, and doubt. Using biblical anecdotes as his brushes, he skillfully sketches illustration after illustration that affirms and assures the reader of God's willingness to restore, replenish and revive.

From marital issues to financial imprisonment; from ministry challenges to infirmity woes, (my favorite was, "Help! Servant Down!), this book addresses the day to day vicissitudes of life; giving concise, pertinent, informative inspiration to contend with and conquer whatever comes our way.

I've always enjoyed curling up with a good book. In this age of microwave intelligence and technology, it is still refreshing to get somewhere quiet and appreciate a 'good read.' This book more than meets that criteria. It is a fascinating work that captivates you quickly and will cause you to ponder, even as you're digesting it, all of the wonderful workings of God in your own personal situations. By the time you reach the book's conclusion, you too will understand that everything you've gone through and bounced back from was all just preparation for you to be everything that God ordained you to be. Good work Dr. Manuel.

+Matthew Marvin Odum, D. Min

Bouncing Back

WHAT DO WE DO WHEN LIFE SEEMS TO BE spiraling out of control? Even with our best effort, our plans tend to fall apart. It's not that we didn't dot every "i" and cross every "t." It's just that life happens. Pain is inevitable. Failure is a part of the process of progress. Misunderstandings arise. People come, and people go. Don't feel strange. Don't perceive yourself or your situation as strange, weird, or even cursed due to the presence of problems; they're normal. And that is the purpose for my writing this book: to help you to dismiss the notion that pain is an anomaly, and disappointment is an abnormality, and most importantly, that faith in God is an escape from the vicissitudes of life. If I may be honest, I would say, "Life is quite the opposite."

Perhaps, one of Satan's favorite lies and the misconception within Christendom today is that individuals who put their trust in God should not experience the ebbs and flows of life. This type of thinking is encapsulated in that all-famous question we often hear and ask: Why do bad things happen to good people? Such a question reveals the flaw in the theology promoted in many churches. This question shows the error found in the philosophies developed in much of the Western hemisphere, and there is a word for this type of attitude, it's Escapism. We would love to escape the pain that growth naturally brings our way. We'd like to avoid and bypass the pressure that progress requires to succeed. I'm sure that we would all love to just soar through life peacefully without ever having to face the tough situations that drive us to our knees in prayer. We'll often pray to God and ask Him to teach us how to be patient, but we become impatient while waiting for this virtue to develop in our lives. We ask God for a godly character, but avoid being placed in positions where our attitudes and beliefs are confronted and changed. We want faith without trials and tribulations. We want paychecks without work. We want to love without sacrifice, and we desire freedom without struggle. Why do bad things happen to good people? The answer is simple; it is on the back of hardship and adversity that greatness is produced.

I love to watch basketball. Basketball is a sport that most people are familiar with or at least, watch on television. Do not worry; you don't have to know how to play basketball to get this principle. You might not even be able to dribble a ball, run down a court without double-dribbling, or toss a layup into a hoop; you might not be able to dunk even on a kiddie goal, but there are some simple rules of the game that can benefit you in life. One of the most important rules in basketball is this: You must dribble the ball to move it from one place on the court to another. Think about that for a moment. Without dribbling the ball, you can't change its location, you can't improve its position, you can't score points, and you certainly cannot win the game. If Michael Jordan, Kevin Durant, Kobe Bryant, LeBron James, Sheryl Swoopes, Allen Iverson, Candace Parker, Stephen Curry, Magic Johnson, Dr. J, or any of the all-time greats of the sport didn't know how to dribble a basketball, their names would not be plastered on the walls of the hall of greatness. What does it mean to dribble? It is here that we find both the irony of success and a consistent pattern in life.

The word "dribble" means "to propel by successive, slight taps or bounces with hand, foot, or stick" (Webster's). In essence, the ball doesn't get moved forward unless it is successively bounced off the ground. As the ball on the court of life, the goal is not to remain on the ground; it's to get back up, over and over again. What a strange but articulate metaphor when you think of the bouncing ball, but therein lies the skill and the ability to maintain control of a bouncing ball. If I had to put my money on the better ball handler, having to choose between Allen Iverson, Stephen Curry, Michael Jordan, or God, I would certainly bet that God is much more capable of handling our bouncing lives than any NBA player could handle a basketball. But do we understand how things work? Do we know that to advance in life, we have to fall and then get back up again, fall and then rise, fall and then jump back up? We can't stay down. We can't give up. We can't lose heart. We have to learn how to get back up again. Naively, most of us have not discovered that victory does not go to the one who avoids falling; it goes to the one who avoids staying down.

If I could be prophetic for one second, I declare in the name of Jesus that your season of stagnation has come to an end. That is why this book is in your hand right now. God has commissioned me to teach you how to get back up after you've stumbled and fallen. Let's get started, shall we?

Why Go Through All Of The Trouble?

WATER WAS RAPIDLY FILLING THE BOAT. RELENTLESS waves, splashing and pounding against the side of the boat, were as vicious as a sadistic and cruel tyrant hell-bent on destruction. At that moment, it seemed as if the weight and wrath of the universe descended on that little fishing boat out in the middle of the Sea of Galilee. There was no one else around to hear their cries, their calls for help. There was no distress signal they could send. The roars of the waves drowned out the sound of their voices. They were helpless. Scared. Desperate. They were like little children who were all alone, sitting in the grip of fear. Only one thing remained stable, unshaken, and unmovable at that moment: it was an idea that rested on all of their minds: *Where is He? Where is Jesus?*

When I ponder the plight of religion today in America and attempt to diagnose the failing spiritual health of many who traverse this land, there is one common thought that fills the hearts of people from all socio-economic backgrounds and ethnicities: the question of God's presence. Many just don't feel as if God is present enough in their affairs. An absent God is not a good God. An indifferent God is a negligent God. So, if God is real, then He must not be as good as some make Him out to be. He is no better than a deadbeat father. This being the sentiments of many people. For others, the seeming lack of God's involvement in their affairs has produced a toxic attitude within them; this attitude manifesting as they spew vitriolic jargon dismissing the very existence of God. One of the world's leading evolutionary scientists, thinkers, and academians, Richard Dawkins, in his international bestselling book, *The God Delusion*, dared express what many people are thinking but are afraid to say due to the taboo placed on such words. In his book, Dawkins called the Christian God "the most unpleasant character in all fiction: jealous and proud of it; a petty, unjust, unforgiving control-freak; a vindictive, bloodthirsty ethnic cleanser; a misogynistic, homophobic, racist, infanticidal, genocidal, filicidal, pestilential, megalomaniacal, sadomasochistic, capriciously malevolent bully."[1] Not too far behind him was the famed philosopher and thinker, Friedrich Wilhelm Nietzsche, who once called Christianity "the one great curse, the one great intrinsic depravity, the one great instinct of revenge, for which no means are venomous enough, or secret, subterranean and small enough . . . . the one immortal blemish upon the human race"[2] and famously claimed, "God is dead."[3] And I can go on and on, filling the book with quotes that demonize and discredit God and religion, but I think you get the point. There are some angry people out there, angry because they feel as if God is an absent, negligent, apathetic, unreliable, undependable figure in their lives, and rather than put their faith in God or even entertain the idea of faith, they would rather dismiss the whole concept altogether and even dismiss faith as "the opium of the people"[4] as Karl Marx once stated. In other words, there is a significant portion of society that looks at Bible readers, those that bend their knees and pray, those that lift their hands during worship services and the likes as delusional people looking for an escape from reality...as if faith is a drug that merely steals our attention while subtly destroying our lives. To them, religion is a disease, and its adherents are suffering from a sickness.

To be honest, Dawkins, Nietzsche, Marx, and all other God-haters have naturally found themselves floating adrift on boats of dreams on the vast ocean of life, asking the same question that the twelve men in that little fishing boat on the Sea of Galilee were asking: Where is God? Perhaps, we could argue that the only difference between the disciples of Christ who were in a state of panic and fear, and the atheists and God-haters who had succumb to fear and panic at some point in their own lives and began doubting God, is that Jesus made Himself known to the disciples during their time of distress—in an incredible display of supernaturalism. Jesus approached the twelve men, walking on the water. Behind such an encounter, who would not be a Believer? But how often does something like this occur? How often does Jesus physically reveal Himself to us? Sadly, not very often. The approach that Christ takes today is the one He took with the Apostle Thomas, where he said to him after appearing to him after His resurrection, "You believe because you have seen me. Blessed are those who believe without seeing me" (John 20:29, New Living Translation).

That's what faith is. Faith believes God without having to see Him physically; it is trusting God without having to have some supernatural occurrence take place indicating God's involvement; it's believing God when He promises to take care of you; more importantly, faith is better defined by what it isn't. Faith isn't the ability to stop storms from arising in life. Faith isn't the ability to manipulate the elements of nature, control the winds, or magically conjure up a fire. Faith isn't some force you can control. Faith is simply your ability to believe and trust God through every situation you encounter. Faith is believing that God will always be there to assist and rescue you in the worst situations, and even perform the miraculous if necessary.

Ironically, everyone places faith in something. The atheist places faith in science, and science puts faith in materialism and unproven theories such as evolution. People claim that an event took place millions of years ago, setting off a chain of events (The Big Bang Theory) that miraculously produced the many complex organisms on the earth today. And yet, the adherents of evolution and Big Bang cosmology weren't there to witness any of these happen. They theorize that the event happened. I don't know about you, but I call that faith—the willingness and ability to believe that which you have not and cannot see. Many of us place confidence in ourselves, believing that we are our gods. But medical crises in our lives quickly disproves this theory.

I have discovered that one of the big questions humanity often harbors within is not a question concerning the existence of God. Rather, most people question the fairness of God in allowing certain things to happen in our world, and it's in light of this question that so many people are struggling with their faith today. The reason bad things occur is the issue I want to tackle in this chapter.

GOD OF THE WIND

I noticed something interesting in Mark chapter 4. In that passage of Scripture, Jesus sent His disciples out to the sea with specific instructions to sail across it to the other side. People commonly believe that hardships and storms come as a result of not doing the right thing. We teach this to our children and then cringe as we see their belief in this lie crumble. We tell them that if they are nice to others, others will be nice to them; that if they do good in school and get their lessons, they will avoid the pitfalls of drugs, alcoholism, addiction, poverty, and homelessness. We tell them that if they say their prayers every night, no bad will come to them. I think Joyce Meyers explained it best that this isn't true. In her testimony, Joyce recalls being molested by her father as a little girl—this abuse continued in her life well into her young adult years. In one instance, Joyce recalls fervently praying to God to deliver her from the hands of her abusive father, only to still suffer through rape that night and the night after, and the night after that. Of course, her big question once an adult and safely positioned outside of that place of torment, was this: Where was God when I needed Him? Put another way: Why didn't God stop the storm from coming?

It's one thing to be in the position where bad things happen to you at random, but it's an entirely different thing when bad things happen to you in the course of walking obediently before God. What many people in the church are not being taught today is that bad things do happen to us when we are in the course of following God's instructions. You may lose a house as a result of obeying God. You may lose a loved one as a result of following God. You might lose your job, your career, your income as a result of obeying God. You might lose friends and even family support as a result of surrendering your life to God. The point is you will, not might experience some loss as a result of doing the right thing. We must get the proper understanding of the way things go so that we can shed the wrong expectations that breed faithlessness and disbelief in the love and power of God.

THE QUESTION OF GOD'S WHEREABOUTS

We have all heard those one-liners before: "If God loved me, He wouldn't have . . ." "How could a loving God allow such a bad thing to happen?" We have all probably said them a time or two. You might be thinking them now. When tragedies such as the shooting that occurred at Sandy Hook Elementary School where over twenty children were gunned down by a homicidal maniac or the Charleston, South Carolina A.M.E. Church shooting where a young Caucasian man gunned down innocent worshipers during a prayer service in hopes of starting a race war take place. The first question on people's minds is Where is God? And to be honest, that's a typical question. I don't think God gets offended when we ask questions. God didn't get mad at the Israelites for wondering about His whereabouts during their four hundred years of captivity in Egypt. God didn't get angry at Joseph for undoubtedly wondering about His whereabouts while he was being bounced around from hardship to hardship, going from slave quarters to a prison cell for over ten years just for having a dream. God didn't get angry at John the Baptist for questioning the legitimacy of Jesus' claim of being the Messiah while he was awaiting execution at the hands of the demented King Herod Antipas while rotting in a dingy dungeon prison cell. God didn't even get angry when His Son, Jesus the Christ, questioned His whereabouts while hanging on the cross - "My God, my God, why hast thou forsaken me?" (Matthew 27:46). It seems like the question of God's whereabouts gets floated around a lot, so don't feel bad if you've found yourself uttering that question a time or two—God is accustomed to hearing it. There is one thing that I have noticed: in each of the examples I stated a moment ago, and I noticed that God never intervened and changed the actual circumstances surrounding those in distress. Instead, He changed their perspectives while they were in the midst of their situations. In essence, what God did was strengthen them to overcome their trials, rather than encourage them to avoid them. Why are tests necessary for us? Simply put, trials and tribulations are the mechanisms that keep us dependent on God and mature our faith. The Bible tells us in James 1 verses 2 and 3, "*Dear brothers and sisters, when troubles come your way, consider it an opportunity for great joy. For you know that when your faith is tested, your endurance has a chance to grow.*"

What a change of perspective!!! Does God expect us to rejoice when bad things hit our lives? Apparently, yes! But who in their right mind would do such a thing? Who would say, "Praise the Lord," after they've lost a job or "Hallelujah," after being diagnosed with cancer? Apparently, the only type of person who would do such a thing is the person who sees trials and tribulations as opportunities to prove God's power and love in their lives. These are individuals who have learned to overcome the hatred, fear, envy, insecurity, bitterness, and confusion that life tried to instill in them as a result of their unfortunate circumstances. They have proven that God can calm the raging seas inside of us even while all hell is busting loose all around us. They have shown that there is no peace like the peace that comes from knowing God. No love like that which enraptures our souls when we bask in God's presence, and no victory like we possess when we refuse to be broken by our external circumstances.

No, the Bible didn't say praise God for the bad things; it told me to praise God in the midst of the turbulent times. In other words, how else can Jesus prove how valuable you are to Him and how powerful He is in our lives if the waves of the sea are not crashing against the sides of our comfortable existence? He has to permit trouble to come, so that He can reveal His power and love. You didn't end up in the storm because God does not love you. You ended up in the storm because God desires to show you and those watching, how deep His love is for you.

One thing we must consider always is this: life on earth is not eternal; it's temporary. The pain we experience is temporary. As James put it, "our lives are like vapors, here one minute and then gone the next." We spend billions of dollars just trying to prolong the lifespan of vapor. We forget that it's our life eternally we should be concerned about—that's where Heaven and Hell come into play. That's why the Apostle Paul urges us in Romans chapter eight to be "spiritual-minded" and focus on the "glory that shall be revealed" in us once we leave this life plane of existence and receive our heavenly bodies. Paul said the pains and sufferings we're experiencing now could not even be "compared" to this future glory. This life is just a test. There is a reward in store for those that pass this test. But the only way to pass this test is to remain spiritually minded by keeping the right perspective. We must remember that our souls are more important than our physical bodies, eternity is endless unlike life here on earth, and that being rejoined to God is more important than gaining all of the earthly possessions there is to gain. So rejoice! Our hardships are drawing us closer to God. Our pain is helping us to turn more to God. Our problems make us pray. Our troubles cause us to put our faith into practice. Challenging situations contribute to shaping our character. It is in light of the truth that Peter was excited about being crucified upside-down, Thomas was glad to risk life and his limb just to preach the Gospel of Jesus the Christ in India, Paul was pleased to be executed by the Romans for the cause of the Gospel. These men, after being enlightened by the truth, were more excited about shedding this life and seeing Heaven, than they were concerned with what goes on down here. They realized that their rewards were going to be great in Heaven because of the things they chose to endure for Christ's sake.

When Christ invites us, He is inviting us to a life of abundance. Jesus told us in John 10 verse 10 that He came to give us life and life more abundantly. With the abundant life that Christ came to give us, we receive God's peace, His joy, His love, a sense of purpose and significance, and we also have the right to healing, deliverance, breakthrough, prosperity, and so much more. Not only does God offer us life in abundance on the earth, but He also provides us with an eternal home in Heaven after we depart from the earth. But there is one thing I can't leave out of this package: included with the abundant life that Christ offers us is the presence of trials and tribulations. In

Mark 10 verse 30, Jesus promised us that when we surrender our all to God, we will be blessed tremendously in return, but along with these blessings will come persecution. Jesus didn't promise us that we'll only see sunny days and flowers; He did promise us some rainy days and thorns also; this is in part due to the fact that our adversary, Satan, hates it when we surrender our lives to Christ and he sets out on a mission to distract us as much as possible by throwing as many problems our way in hopes of discouraging us, making us lose sight of God, and even making us doubt God. The Bible does tell us in the Book of Revelation, the twelfth chapter, that Satan has come down with great wrath because he knows his time is short. This means you can expect as much trouble from him as possible because he doesn't have much time left before he meets his end. But realize that Satan is not after your money, your house, your car, or your health; he's after your faith. This is what Peter reveals to us in 1 Peter 5 verses 8 and 9: "Be sober, be vigilant; because your adversary the devil, as a roaring lion, walketh about, seeking whom he may devour: Whom resist steadfast in the faith, knowing that the same afflictions are accomplished in your brethren that are in the world."

Trust me; everything that's happening in your life is the cause of either building your faith or robbing you of your faith.

Are there waves raging in your life right now? Are the billows from the turbulent waters of life beating against the side of your existence? Know that Jesus placed you in those waters for a reason. You're not where you are by accident. God is up to something in your life. He's getting ready to reveal Himself to you and others through your situation in an extraordinary way. Just be patient and know that He has His eyes on you. If you look close enough, the same way Jesus walked on water to get to the disciples, he has done the same thing for you. That's why your situation has not consumed you. That's why your marriage has not ended in divorce. That's why your kids are still alive despite the enemy's constant attack because Jesus is in the water with you. So get up, shake yourself off, and declare to the enemy, "I will get back up again!"

GET BACK UP

CHAPTER TWO

Pushing Pass
My Parents' Mess

ONE OF THE MOST RESEARCHED TOPICS IN THE WORLD is the effects of parenting on children. Thousands of books have been written by psychologists and mental health experts on this subject. For example, one study I found explains the effects of substance abuse by parents on their children: "Today, researchers from Harvard Medical School (HMS) announced new findings that children whose parents (or caregivers) abuse alcohol—or use, produce or distribute drugs—face significantly higher risks of medical and behavioral problems, including substance abuse."[1]

In another study by the Journal of Clinical Child and Adolescent Psychology, we find that "higher levels of harsh-negative parenting is related to higher levels of depressive symptoms"[2] in children. In layman's terms, what this means is children whose parents tend to be critical and harsh towards them, rather than supportive of them, tend to suffer more with depression. There were studies conducted by researchers that revealed the negative effects of divorce on children's behavior, the consequences of not touching and showing affection to infants, and how this damages their mental development and even stunts their physical development, and more. The main point of all of these studies is this: The foundation of a child's life is laid by the parent; the parent can either set their child up for success or failure by their actions.

If you're a parent and you're thinking that your actions aren't affecting your child in some way, think again. Your child sees all that you do and processes all that they see mentally, and they ponder things in their souls that they often conceal behind the walls of silence.

Do you want your child to develop an attitude of distrust towards others? Well, keep making promises to them and not keeping them. Do you want your child to become self-centered and think that they are supposed to always get what they want? Well, keep giving them everything they want. And even when you do say "no" to them, give in to their demands after they've thrown a temper tantrum and hissy fit. If you want your child to disrespect authority, then keep putting off disciplining them after they've brought home those bad grades and bad reports from their teachers. In fact, while you're at it, why don't you just march up to the school and curse the teacher out the next time they give your child a bad report; that will reinforce in that child's mind that they don't need to respect anyone else's authority, including your own. Do you want your little girl to strive to be promiscuous? Well, keep modeling promiscuity in front of her. And while you are at it, why don't you continue playing vile and vulgar music and show her how to "twerk" as a parent. I'm sure she will get the message. Furthermore, if you want your child to shun God and church, then be a hypocrite in front of them: only act one way in church and an entirely different way outside of the church while they're watching. They'll register this message in their minds: Church is just an act. It's not real.

THE CARDINAL RULE

I'm sure most of us have heard our parents say at one time or another, "Do as I say, not as I do!" But here is a cardinal rule: Children follow what you do, not what you say. Children significantly learn through observation. Don't we all? The Apostle Paul, in 1 Corinthians 11 verse 1, revealed to us the primary method he used to teach new converts to the Christian faith how to conduct themselves. He wrote, "Be ye followers of me, even as I also am of Christ."

I like the way the New American Standard Bible says it: "Be imitators of me, just as I also am of Christ."

To imitate someone just means to copy everything they do, to follow them as a model. If you have played the game Simon Says, then I'm sure you're familiar with the principle of imitation. The goal of imitation is not to understand, analyze, figure out, or even make sense of what someone else is doing; it's just to do what they're doing. Successful people have learned one fundamental principle in life: Just do what other successful people have done and you'll reap the same results in your own life; find someone successful and glean from their example.

Jesus modeled faith in front of His disciples for three and a half years while on the earth so that they could imitate

Him. Essentially, whenever Jesus would rebuke His disciples for lack of faith, He was scolding them for their unwillingness to imitate what they had seen Him model out in front of them.

What are you modeling in front of your child? When you get in a jam, do they see you doubting God or do they see you girding yourself up in faith and standing on God's promises? When you get upset about something, do your children see you kicking and punching holes in the walls, or do they see you responsibly managing your emotions? What your kids see you do is ultimately the model they're going to imitate. The Apostle Peter urged leaders in the church in 1 Peter 5 verse 3, "Don't lord it over the people assigned to your care, but lead them by your good example."

In other words, Peter was explaining, as did the Apostle Paul, that real leadership is modeling out the behavior you want others to follow. You do it first as a leader, and then let the people follow your example. This explains what is meant by the saying that goes; the people will take on the spirit of the leader. As a leader, whether in the home, the workplace, the church, or even the classroom, you greatly determine the type of attitude the people in that environment will possess.

GROWING UP IN A DESERT

Regarding bad parenting, there's probably no greater example of this than the ancient Israelites in the Old Testament. To put it mildly, the ancient Israelites set a horrible example for the generations that followed after them. Numbers chapter thirteen details the deeds of these people, revealing where and how they failed to accomplish the will of God for their lives. So bad was the example set by these Israelites that God warned future generations of Believers not to follow in their ways in the book of Hebrews chapters three and four:

> "Today when you hear his voice, don't harden your hearts as Israel did when they rebelled, when they tested me in the wilderness. There your ancestors tested and tried my patience, even though they saw my miracles for forty years. So I was angry with them, and I said, 'Their hearts always turn away from me. They refuse to do what I tell them.' So in my anger I took an oath: 'They will never enter my place of rest.' Be careful then, dear brothers and sisters. Make sure that your own hearts are not evil and unbelieving, turning you away from the living God" (New Living Translation).

The Israelites made God so angry that He allowed them to wander in a desert for forty years. Think about that. What was supposed to be a two-week journey got turned into a forty-year journey because of the actions of these people? Because of the decisions of the parents, the children were born in a desert as opposed to the Promised Land (a fertile land containing all of the necessities of life and more). When parents don't strive to improve the circumstances in their own lives, they place their children at an unfair disadvantage in life. The sons and daughters of the Israelites had to grow up in a dry, dead, barren land because of their parents. One of the main reasons why so many youths are trapped in the web of drugs and wallowing in poverty and even hopelessness today is because of the environments they're growing up in. Many young people, when they look at their surroundings, all they see in their neighborhoods are drugs, prostitution, gangs, and crime; so, the likelihood that they would gravitate towards these things is a little bit greater than those not growing up in these environments. If the youth in these environments are not exposed to a higher level of living, they may just run the risk of thinking what they see is all life has to offer. Placing the youth in a better environment may not change their character, but it will expose them to something greater, which, in turn, may just inspire them to transform their behaviors so that they can obtain greater things in life.

If you are growing up in a desert, know that there is so much more that life has to offer you; know that there is a Promised Land around the corner that has a spot reserved in it just for you. Where you are is not where you have to stay. God has a better life for you.

WHAT NOT TO DO

What did the Israelites do that caused them to lose the blessings of God in their lives, and consequently, cause their children to experience a forty-year setback in life? Here are a few things:

1. They doubted God's Word. It is important to note that when we doubt God's Word, we will set ourselves up for failure, but not only ourselves; we also train our children to question God as well, which will only set them up for failure in their own lives. The Bible tells us to meditate on God's Word day and night, and we will make our own way prosperous in life (Joshua 1:8). Prosperity comes when we align ourselves with God's Word. Biblical prosperity doesn't merely consist of financial blessings, but it also consists of good health, peace, joy, favor with men, a good reputation, and more; and furthermore, bib-

lical prosperity puts our children in a position where they will have an advantage in life. Psalm 112 verses 1-3 declares, "How joyful are those who fear the LORD and delight in obeying his commands. Their children will be successful everywhere; an entire generation of godly people will be blessed. They will be wealthy, and their good deeds will last forever" (New Living Translation).

It is important that we teach our children to turn to God, pray, believe and trust His Word in their lives. Depending on God is the only way they are going to succeed in their own lives. And you may be asking, "What about people who are successful that don't believe in God and go to church?" Well, Jesus revealed to us that real prosperity and success goes deeper than the physical when He asked in Mark 8 verse 36, "For what shall it profit a man, if he shall gain the whole world, and lose his own soul?"

If the only thing you have is material wealth, but you lack a sincere a relationship with God, then you will still have a void in your soul. A space in your heart that will leave you feeling empty inside; and even worse is when you die, not only will you still leave your material possessions behind, but your eternal destination will be Hell. And when you consider this fact, you find out that life is too short and eternity is too long to fathom, and you should be more concerned about the state of your soul than the state of your bank account.

2. The children of Israel disobeyed God's instructions. The Israelites had been instructed by God to go into the Land of Canaan and possess it, but they rebelled and decided to do their own thing instead. It is interesting how the parents' disobedi-

ence towards God placed the children at a disadvantage in their lives. When God tells us to do something, He is thinking about not only our blessings, but also the blessings our children will reap as a result of our obedience. Imagine if Joseph had disobeyed the command of the angel to leave town when Jesus was just an infant—there's a good chance Jesus would have been murdered by the authorities while just a baby, thereby losing the opportunity to die on the cross for our sins. So many people choose sin over God and reap disaster over their households as a result thereof. Because of the choice that was made to sin over obeying God, adultery has destroyed families and left the children out in the cold, confused, fearful, and discouraged in life. Because of the choice to steal, rob, and commit murder, families, and lives are left shattered and bruised. Due to the decision to not obey God in the area of our finances by tithing and being good stewards of God's money, we end up forfeiting blessings that would have benefited our entire households. Because we hold on to unforgiveness, hatred, and grudges, our children often find themselves being swept up in the winds of conflict, injustice, racism, and class warfare. Leaving them to become victims of these things, even to the point of experiencing generational curses that keep violence, hatred and death in their households for years to come. Don't be like the Israelites and sin, and be disobedient towards God. Remember that sin will always look good to you for a season, but its result will be death and destruction.

YOU CAN BREAK THE CURSE

I sometimes wish I had one of those beautiful childhood stories that so many others have, but that does not describe my upbringing. It sure would have been nice to be raised in a household with two Jesus-loving parents who modeled the right way to live before me, but that's not what I experienced growing up. I had two parents like any other child, but they were not married, stable, or mature. To be honest, my parents conceived me at a time when a child should have been the last thing on their minds; my father was only eighteen, and my mother was just sixteen. Coupled with the fact that they were not married and children themselves with being broke, and add a child to the mix, and you get a surefire appointment to doom and gloom for them and me. Though the plan of the enemy and the statistics may have determined that I would not amount to anything, God had another plan for my life. And can I tell you something, though your upbringing may not have been ideal, God does have a plan for your life. As a matter of fact, versus you murmuring and complaining about how bad your situation is or how terrible your parents were; you need to push past the pain and seek God for your purpose. Because it is in your purpose, where you will discover your true happiness. Not in your parents hugging you as a child, kissing you on your forehead, or walking you to school. The enemy knows that God has a plan to prosper you, he keeps reminding you of how much love and affection you lacked as a child, and he uses your anger and resentment towards your parents to keep you anchored in the place called going nowhere. Now I know this trick all too well, because I fell for the enemy's bait for a large part of my life by resenting my parents. And the crazy thing about this type of behavior is that it has the potential if left unresolved, to serve as a convenient excuse for anyone entangled in the enemy's web of destruction to accept failure and defeat in everything they attempt to do in life. So stop vilifying your parents for their shortcomings. Yes, they made mistakes. Yes, they did not give you the love and affection you deserved. And yes, you are correct; they may have been terrible parents. But before you condemn them, please take time to investigate why God chose them to bring you into the world. Remember, He is God, and he could have picked any man and woman in the world to be your parents, but he selected them. That's right, those young, unmarried, broke and unstable people, known as your biological parents, were God's selection. And he did it because they provided the perfect ecosystem for you to become all that He predestined you to be.

Truthfully, what may seem like a curse was a blessing in disguise. In my case, with my parents being so young and unprepared for parenthood, my grandparents were able to fill a void in my life by providing love and stability during my formative years (my parents were not absentee, they were merely young). And I am sure if you looked close enough, even if it was for a short time or from a person that you often overlooked, God put somebody in your life to give you inspiration and hope.

The Bible tells us in the book of Proverbs that a wise child will pursue after knowledge and understanding and seek after the instructions of the wise. You may not have a stable source of wisdom in your household, but I guarantee you there is someone close that God has planted as an undercover agent to nurture you the right way; it might be a teacher, a neighbor, a mother at your church, or your spouse. Instead of pushing them away or avoiding them, give that person a chance to love you because they are God sent. For me, after the death of my grandparents, I lived with my Mother until I was thirteen and then with my father until I was eighteen. Though they provided the necessities of life for me as best they could, neither of them were saved during my time with them. For this reason, God ordained me a Godmother, Mama Net, who filled this void by taking me to church and introduced me to God.

Honestly, I did not come to grips with this all-important revelation until I was twenty-nine years old. At which point, my back was against the wall, my marriage was on the fritz, and I had fathered a child out of wedlock myself. One thing is for sure, if I did not give my life to Christ when he called, my anger and resentment for my parent's was going to continue being my achilles heel in life. So for the sack of Christ, my future, and the hope of becoming a better husband and parent, I had to do the same thing you must do now, let it go. Yes, it is possible to do the opposite of that which your parents have done. It is possible for you to rise above your environment. But it can only happen with the help of God.

In the book of Numbers, two men behaved differently from the rest of the Israelites and experienced success where their parents had failed: Joshua and Caleb. The Bible says these two men had "a different spirit" than the rest of the people, meaning their attitudes were different. Their willingness to be different goes to show that everyone around you can have a bad attitude and the wrong outlook on life, but you can still have the right attitude and outlook on life. Joshua and Caleb were the only individuals over the age of twenty that made it into the Promised Land. Why? Because they chose to see things differently from the rest of the people; they opted to see things God's way rather than man's way; they decided that it was better to fear God and obey His commandments rather than fear public opinion and follow the flesh.

Imagine this: Out of over two million people in the desert, only two men possessed the right attitude and were allowed to enter into the Promised Land with the next generation. Just two. If you're reading this book right now, you're one of the individuals God has ordained to be a curse-breaker in your household. God is cultivating within you a different perspective and attitude even now. You are getting ready to set a new standard, experience greater things, do greater things, and walk into a new season of blessings. Declare this over your life today!

Your parents' shortcomings do not have to mess up your future and rob you of God's promises. In fact, God is going to use you to rewrite the script of your parents' mess if you let Him. When I look at my situation now, it's unbelievable that I'm blessed to serve in my God-given purpose in life, having a happy marriage, a great son, and blessed with a stable lifestyle. My life displays the Promise Land that God promised to those who follow Him, and I'm blessed to experience this phase of my life with my parents. My mother, who is an awesome woman of God, was blessed to rewrite her life extraordinarily. Though she started as an unwed teenage mother who dropped out of high school, she earned a G.E.D. while working at night, after which she attended and graduated from college. Currently, she works in the field of her dreams as a medical assistant, and she is a licensed minister. In the same manner, my father retired from the Army National Guard and currently serves as a deacon. In a further display of the hand of God on his life, he was blessed to marry the love of his life, affectionately known as Mama J.

Together, they are the proud owners of G & J cleaning service. With a life that I have been called to live and the love I have discovered for my parents, I can testify to the veracity of this statement: You can push past the mess. If you're ready to start, then pray this short prayer with me:

Lord, Jesus, I thank you that you are in my life. I completely surrender to You. Thank you for saving me and making me a brand new creation. My sins are forgiven, and I have been washed in Your blood. I thank You that You have broken the curse of sin and death off of my life. I thank You that I am free from generational curses today. Give me a clean heart and the right attitude. Let my thoughts align themselves with Your Word. I choose to believe Your Word. I agree with Your Word today. I thank You that everything the devil stole from my family and I by way of inheritance will be released unto me. For I declare blessings, deliverance, salvation, prosperity, healing, and righteousness over my household. I thank You, Lord, that despite my parent's shortcomings, I can get back up again with you. In Jesus name, Amen.

Get Back Up

CHAPTER THREE

Release From Financial Prison

THERE IS A FAMOUS SAYING MANY PEOPLE LIKE TO QUOTE: *Money can't buy you happiness*. Well, that's true. Money can't provide you with happiness...but neither can poverty. What can poverty do for you? How happy can you be wondering whether or not you'll be able to put food on the table for your family? How happy can you be not being able to provide the necessities of life for yourself and your family members? I've never seen anyone be happy and content with poverty and financial hardship. No, not one person!

People love to utter the quote I mentioned when they are attempting to justify their financial situation. Unfortunately, many people try to justify their financial situation rather than change it. Some people have become so discouraged due to their hardship that they've accepted defeat as the only way to live. When we accept defeat, we give up on the hope of a better day.

In the Bible, poverty was never considered to be a sign of nobility and righteousness; it was never something to be celebrated; actually, poverty was and is found in God's Word to be a curse. Yes, you read that correctly, a curse! But you do not have to take my word, read these passages for yourself.

2 Corinthians 8 verse 9: "You know the generous grace of our Lord Jesus Christ. Though he was rich, yet for your sakes, he became poor, so that by his poverty he could make you rich." (New Living Translation).

Proverbs 22 verse 7: "Just as the rich rule the poor, so the borrower is servant to the lender." (New Living Translation).

Proverbs 10 verse 4: "Lazy people are soon poor; hard workers get rich." (New Living Translation).

Proverbs 13 verse 18: "If you ignore criticism, you will end in poverty and disgrace; if you accept correction, you will be honored" (New Living Translation)

Deuteronomy 28 verses 1-6 and verses 15-18: "If you fully obey the LORD your God and carefully keep all his commands that I am giving you today, the LORD your God will set you high above all the nations of the world. You will experience all these blessings if you obey the LORD your God: Your towns and your fields will be blessed. Your children and your crops will be blessed. The offspring of your herds and flocks will be blessed. Your fruit baskets and breadboards will be blessed. Wherever you go and whatever you do, you will be blessed. . . 'But if you refuse to listen to the LORD your God and do not obey all the commands and decrees I am giving you today, all these curses will come and overwhelm you: Your towns and your fields will be cursed. Your fruit baskets and breadboards will be cursed. Your children and your crops will be cursed. The offspring of your herds and flocks will be cursed" (New Living Translation).

Many more Bible verses reveal to us that poverty is not designed by God to be a part of His people's lives, but I'll stop right there. I think you get the point.

Notice what the Bible says about poverty and its causes: poverty is a result of the curse that Adam and Eve caused to enter into the earth through their disobedience. Poverty places us in slavery and often is a result of laziness. Poverty is also caused by pride, arrogance, and the unwillingness to listen to wisdom and receive instruction and correction in life. Lastly, poverty is a curse that God brought upon His people for their disobedience and sinfulness. There is nowhere in Scripture where poverty was a reward given by God to an individual who obeyed His voice and followed His instructions. Yes, as a Christian, you may have to go through seasons where you'll experience meager means, but even then, God still supplies all of our needs. As David put it in Psalm 37 verse 25, "I was young, and now I am old; yet have I not seen the righteous forsaken, nor his seed begging bread" (New King James Version).

Maybe all of your wants or desires of the flesh may not

be given by God, but when you are obedient to his will, his way and his word, your needs will be met. When you follow God's plan for your life, your beginnings may be small, but your latter days will be filled with abundant blessings that will ultimately trickle down to your descendants. Rather than passing down a generational curse of poverty, those who obey God's voice will pass down generational blessings.

SERVING HARD TIME

Financial hardship doesn't feel like a prison; it is a prison. Living paycheck to paycheck causes insomnia, nightmares, and irritability. One's worst fear when stuck in the world's system of robbing Peter to pay Paul or living payday to payday, is to lose their source of income, get fired from their job, lose a contract, take a major blow to their career, etc. When the Great Recession of 2007 hit the United States, many families found themselves struggling just to survive. Depression skyrocketed. Suicide rates climbed. So many people during this time lost their homes, their marriages, and seemingly lost their way. Tiffiny and I had first-hand experience regarding these difficult times. In fact, during the Recession, we got to a point in which we could no longer afford to pay our mortgage, so our mortgage company filed a foreclosure order. Now, this may not have been a state of physical incarceration, but if you have ever been in the grip of this type of desperation that poverty brings, then you know poverty is a state of mental imprisonment. Poverty will keep you locked in a state of fear and anxiety, and it will make you feel worthless.

You may be serving hard time in the financial prison I have described right now. I don't know, only you know. But the one thing I want you to recognize right now is poverty is not God's plan for your life. Don't let anyone tell you otherwise. There's a difference between going through a valley and a person building a house in the valley. Because houses are built in places for people to stay long term, but living permanently in the valley was never God's plan for the Believer. As a Christian, you may be going through a tough situation right now, but keep your head up and realize that you are only passing through. You're not designed to die in the wilderness. There is a Promised Land reserved just for you. Don't settle for where you are. Don't defend a curse. Don't attempt to justify something that is not a part of God's plan for your life. Anticipate greater. It's on the way! However, I must inform you of a crucial fact, during your valley experience, there are some important lessons you have to learn if you're going to escape from the financial prison of the world. I had to learn these things. Someone had to sit me and my wife down and teach us proper stewardship principles so that we could make wise decisions with our money and climb out of the pit of poverty and paycheck-to-paycheck living we allowed ourselves to get caught in. To be honest, it was not easy for me to make the changes necessary for us to get up out of my financial slump. Making adjustments in one's lifestyle is one of the most difficult tasks; it requires lots of discipline, which is something most people don't want to exercise. Despite the seemingly insurmountable financial difficulties my wife and I faced, we were sick and tired of living in the hog pen, so we set our sights on the Promise Land. Because I know that you are tired of living beneath your God-given ability, I want to share with you what we learned and help you get out of financial prison:

STEPS TO BREAKING OUT OF FINANCIAL PRISON

1. Ask God to bless you financially: My wife and I were sinking in debt. We were drowning due to our financial situation, and with stress came tension, anxiety, and depression. Thank God we knew how to do one thing when we didn't know what else to do, call on God for help. And that's just what we did. My wife and I had to do the simplest thing first, join hands together, come together on one accord, and ask God to give us direction. According to Matthew 7 verse 7, "If we ask and it shall be given" (King James Version).

2. Seek Godly mentorship and guidance: After taking the first step towards changing our financial situation (which was to ask God for help), God began to order our steps in the right direction. The first thing God did was He brought us under the mentorship of a great man of God who could teach us the biblical principles for handling money. Now, this was not easy because we had to leave everything that we knew and move from the United States to Germany to be in the presence of Bishop J. Alan Neal. Though he was a hard leader, Bishop Neal poured truth into our lives and ministry, and taught my wife and I about the importance of honoring God with our finances. While Bishop Neal was demonstrating these principles to us in word and deed, my wife and I were amazed at how ignorant we were at the most basic principles of stewardship. As the Bible tells us in the book of Hosea, people perish due to "a lack of knowledge" of divine principles and religious laws. Learning the divine principles and laws that God has established in the earth will place us in the position to reap wealth and prosperity.

The first divine law Bishop Neal explained to my wife and I was Tithing.

3. Practice the law of tithing: What is tithing? Tithing is the practice of paying a tithe (a tenth of one's income) to someone else; in our case, as Christians, we are to pay our tithes to God through His house, the church. For example, if you made $100 on your paycheck, a tenth of that is $10. Your tithe would only be $10. The Bible tells us in the Book of Deuteronomy 14 verse 23, "Bring this tithe to the designated place of worship—the place the LORD your God chooses for his name to be honored—and eat it there in his presence. This applies to your tithes of grain, new wine, olive oil, and the firstborn males of your flocks and herds. Doing this will teach you always to fear the LORD your God" (New Living Translation).

Notice here that the tithe was to go to the "designated place of worship," which means the house of God. Today, what is the designated place of worship in Christendom? The church. You are not supposed to give your tithe away to charity, or give it to someone on the street, pay bills with it, or spend it on yourself. You are supposed to give your tithe to the church where you belong. In the book of Malachi chapter three, God warned the Israelites that by not tithing, they were robbing Him, stealing from Him. Why is this so? Because the tithe is that which is holy, and therefore, belongs to God. And God furthermore explained to the Israelites that because they "robbed" Him, He was going to curse them. The curse that God promised to bring upon the Israelites was one where their source of income, their source of blessings would be overcome by "the devourer." In this case, God would allow bugs (locusts, cankerworms, etc.) to eat up their harvests, leaving them with no food to feed their families. On the flip-side of this, God's promise to the Israelites was that if they honored Him with their tithes and offerings, He would protect their interests from those pesky insects. With his protection, the children of Israel would have plenty of food to last them, and all of their hard work would not go to waste. Likewise, when we tithe to God's house, God promises to protect our interests so our income will be secured and overflow.

Another thing I want to point out here is that the tithe was to train God's people to fear Him (by "fear," the Bible means to "respect" God). In other words, the reason God wants us to tithe is so that we can honor and recognize Him always, putting Him first, and acknowledging that He and He alone is our source of blessings. When we don't tithe, we are saying to God that He is not our sole source of blessings, that He is not in total control of our lives, and that He is not God of our lives. God desires to be the lord (owner) of all, or not lord at all. God will never share His throne with another person or thing.

I would like to add this for those who may be skeptical of the practice of tithing today and only view it as a Levitical practice that was instituted by the law of Moses. In Genesis 14 verses 18-20, Abraham whom we are the descendants of, tithes to a righteous king, Melchizedek. In other words, the practice of tithing far predated the law of Moses, and is therefore still a practice instituted by God today.

4. Sow what God placed in your possession: In the Old Testament, we find the stories of two different widows who, during

a time of great economic suffering, were able to prosper financially due to the fact that they discovered that the key to their economic freedom was sitting in their own houses, right beneath their noses. In 1 Kings chapter seventeen, there's a story of a widow who, during a drought that was ravishing the land, had only a short supply of meal left to create some food for her and her son to eat. They were now looking at the last of their food supplies when God sent the prophet Elijah to their house to get something to eat. What audacity? How dare a man of God to go to a poor woman's house and ask for the last little bit of food that she possessed? Doesn't he have any consideration for others, especially for those who are already in need? Notice that God sent the prophet there. Also, notice that God had already spoken to the widow's heart about blessing the man of God with her last. It is important to remember that on the other side of obedience to God's instructions are bountiful blessings. You just have to obey God and stop listening to the voice of fear while it tries to remind you of the many reasons why you shouldn't obey God at the precise moment of His calling. When God asks you to make a sacrifice and sow seed to Him, He's doing so because He has a blessing He's about to drop into your hands.

The poor widow obeyed the prophet's instructions, sowed the seed, and experienced a miracle in return. As she fixed the prophet some food, God supernaturally replenished her supplies until her jugs ran over. By the time God supernaturally finished filling up her jugs, she had enough food for her and her son to outlast the drought. The miracle is in the fact that God used what the widow had in her possession to bless her with. All this woman had to do was release what she had in her possession to God, rather than hold onto it out of fear. Whatever seed you sow into God's hands, He can multiply it.

Just as God blessed the woman in 1 Kings chapter seventeen, He blessed another widow in 2 Kings chapter four. This lady was in an unfortunate predicament as well. She was swamped in debt and didn't have the money to pay, and as a result, the creditors were on their way to take her sons into slavery as payment for her debts. This woman needed a miracle, and fast. Just like before, God sent a prophet to this woman's house. When the prophet Elisha arrived, the woman issued her complaint to him about her situation. The prophet then asked her this one simple question, "what do you have in your house?" (2 Kings 4:2). What's in your house? What did God give you to make money with? What is your gift? It doesn't matter how big or small it is, as long as you put it in God's hands, He can do wonders with it and bless your life through it. What do you have? Can you sing, dance, write music, write poetry, work good with numbers, communicate well with others, cook, tell jokes, draw, paint, design things, decorate rooms, sew clothes, motivate others, listen well, help others, fix things, organize things, or strategize well? What has God given you to use that you are not using? Sometimes, we slave away on our jobs while daydreaming about a better life, while overlooking the fact that God has placed inside of every one of us a gift that is meant to be shared with the world. The key, however, is to take that gift which God has blessed you with and submit it to Him, not use it for the world. Only when your gift, your talent, your ability rests in the hands of God can it become extraordinary.

5. Exercise Responsibility: The last thing Bishop Neal taught my wife and I was the importance of being responsible with the money God gave us. Unfortunately, many people come into possession of money without having the knowledge of how to handle money. When we do not know how to manage money, we will squander it and waste it on unnecessary things. This is why a person can win millions of dollars through the lottery and end up broke a year or two later.

What should you do with your money? You should do as the prophet instructed the widow to do in 2 Kings chapter four and pay off your debts. Make sure that you get out of debt before anything. Secondly, cut back on wasteful spending. Don't buy things just because your flesh wants them right then and there. Control your urges. Learn to save more than you spend and live a responsible life. And lastly, learn to save money. We should endeavor to live lives that honor God and allow us to leave an inheritance for our children's children. As the old saying goes, "It takes money to make money." Invest in a business and prepare your kids to expand the businesses you start. Establish multiple streams of income and teach your children to be responsible over the blessings that God releases over your family. And always remember this greatest piece of financial advice that Tiffiny and I were privileged to discover, "be wise, but don't stop sowing."

Lastly, I know someone reading this chapter is asking the million dollar question, what happened with the foreclosure notice on your house? The answer is simple, God! After working these principles for only a few months during the process, God intervened. Not only did we keep our home; our mortgage company forgave the $14,000 debt and dropped our interest rate, which lowered our mortgage payment by $200 a month. Now if I were preaching, I would tell you to touch your neighbor and tell them, "now that's a miracle." Since I'm not preaching and this is merely the closing to this chapter, I will end by saying, "you can get out of financial prison!"

CHAPTER FOUR

All You Need Is Love

ME AND TIFFINY WERE SITTING IN A TREE, k-i-s-s-i-n-g. First came love, then came marriage, but only after a few months, then came the madness. In less than a year's time, my wife, Tiffiny, and I went from experiencing marital bliss to going through a marital nightmare. We went from hugs and kisses, me fathering a child, to military deployment, adultery, to a mutual separation. Before the end of our first year of marriage, my wife and I were already seeking a divorce. We were in a marriage freefall.

WHEN THEY SAY, "ALL YOU NEED IS LOVE."
As I mentioned in a previous chapter, Tiffiny and I did not have a good example of marriage set before us growing up. My parents were in a relationship for a short period during my infancy, although they were never married. Tiffiny's story is similar to mine. She was conceived by unwed teenage parents as well. Coupled with the fact that neither set of our parents were

saved, so we did not even have anyone to point us to the Word of God for help. With no example to follow, painstakingly, we did what we thought was right in our sight.

Tiffiny and I thought, as so many people think today, that all it takes to create a happy home is love. Well, that might be the case, but where most people fail in their understanding is in identifying what love is. Just ask the average person what they think love is and listen to their answers: Love is an emotion. Love is a good feeling that you get about someone. Love is when you choose to be committed to someone no matter what. Love is... In many cases, it will sound as if people are repeating the lyrics to Al Green's classic, "Love and Happiness" song. That's a good song, but when it comes to the biblical definition of love, that song does not quite cover it. Here is the Bible's definition of love:

"But anyone who does not love does not know God, for God is love."—1 John 4: 8 (New King James Version)

Well, that pretty much explains things. That explains where Tiffiny and I went wrong. That explains where our parents went wrong. That explains where the majority of people, in general, go wrong. Love is not an emotion; it's God's presence, His essence, His very being. So, there is a straightforward formula here, if you don't have God, then you don't have genuine love; but if you do have God, then you do have real love. Tiffiny and I had no relationship with God when we first got married. I was in the Army. I was not involved with church, and I was not spending any time with God away from the church. I knew nothing of God's Word, and neither did Tiffiny. With this being the case, both me and Tiffiny were walking in error and doing all of the wrong things together. Neither of us truly knew how to communicate our love for one another. Neither of us understood the principle of forgiveness and what it does in our lives when we operate in it. Neither of us knew how to pray sincerely. Neither of us had a relationship with the Holy Spirit who could hold us accountable individually for our actions; and as a result, we spent more time listening to family members who reminded us of the other's faults. Rather than allowing God to shine the light on our own actions so that we could work on ourselves, rather than trying to change and transform each other, we spiraled out of control. Tiffiny did not understand the law of honor, which is important in marriage; and I did not understand the nature of love. Therefore, I could not love her "as Christ loves the church" because I did not have a personal relationship with the Savior. Two ignorant people who are trying to make a marriage work are like a person trying to drive a car that has no tires or engine. Tiffiny and I could not understand why we could not get anywhere in life, despite our feelings for each other. And as far as that "feeling" that we often mistake for love, we began to realize that we had no idea what it really meant. By the end of our first year of marriage, we were on life support, and the machine was the only thing working in our relationship. Well, I take that back. We did have feelings, but feelings were not going to save this marriage, this was a case for Jesus.

Another thing about love that many people fail to understand is its characteristics. To better illustrate this point, we will look at 1 Corinthians 13 verses 4-7, "Love is patient and kind. Love is not jealous or boastful, proud or rude. It does not demand its own way. It is not irritable, and it keeps no record of being wronged. It does not rejoice about injustice but rejoices whenever the truth wins out. Love never gives up, never loses faith, is always hopeful, and endures through every circumstance" (New Living Translation).

So, let's look at some keywords here. Patient? How many people exercise patience with their spouse? We have a hard enough time being patient with ourselves. In our microwave generation, we demand that everything moves at the speed of sound and happens when we snap our fingers. We want our children to grow up overnight—we even put them in excellerator programs at school so they can get smart quicker. We tell God to hurry up and come during our church services, then check the clock the whole time He is there.

How about the other characteristics listed such as kindness? The word "kindness" means "of a sympathetic or helpful nature" (Webster's). That word sounded like a foreign language to me when I first got married. I had no sympathy, and I had no intentions of delaying my plans to focus on the needs of others. I expected Tiffiny to climb aboard and roll at the speed that I set for us. Nowhere in my mind did I intend to delay my plans and ambitions for the sake of my wife. I figured she better run with me or she would be left behind. Other descriptions include love not being jealous and envious (oh, boy. I need not even try to tackle this one), nor boastful and proud (pride is defined as feeling you are more important or better than other people according to Webster. Is it possible that many of us feel as if we are better than our partners because we have more money, education, or privileges? I know I did), nor rude (Webster defines this as "offensive in manner or action; discourteous"), it doesn't demand its own way (which means love doesn't try to force people to submit to it; it simply gives people the freedom to choose their own way), it isn't irritable (which Webster defines as "easily angered and annoyed." So, when we are quick to get annoyed by our partners and get angry at them, we are not demonstrating love towards them), it keeps no record of others' wrongs (which basically means love doesn't hold grudges and plot revenge, even acting out against others through passive-aggressive behaviors); and lastly, love is always hopeful; it refuses to give up on seeing others delivered, set free, and blessed; and love never loses faith in God's ability to save and bless others. That's what love is like. That's what I was not like. Tiffiny was not like that either. We violated all of these principles and then wondered why our marriage was a wreck.

It is true that to make a marriage work—or any relationship for that matter—all you need is love, but that's only if you know what love is. With the characteristics mentioned a moment ago, every relationship would thrive because we would have selfless, considerate, understanding, forgiving, gentle, patient, sympathetic, helpful, humble, respectful, optimistic, always encouraging our spouse, while joyfully participating in their lives. And if that's not enough, by having God's presence in our lives and His Spirit operating in us, we will also have the Fruit of the Spirit working in our hearts. This means we will have on top of love and its characteristics these extra attributes: joy, peace, longsuffering, kindness, goodness, faithfulness, gentleness, and self-control (Galatians 5:22-23). Who couldn't appreciate having someone with all of these wonderful characteristics to spend the rest of their lives with?

I did not understand that to love Tiffiny "as Christ loves the church" meant to display each of the characteristics as mentioned above in our relationship. I may have been displaying some of these characteristics, but I was certainly not demonstrating all of them. Neither one of us were walking in the love that God declares in his Word, and because of our ignorance and disobedience, our marriage experienced this great freefall.

LOVING THROUGH THE PAIN

Some people may claim they are too hurt to love anyone else; that they have been burned one too many times by others they put their trust in. Well, we must consider that the very God whose nature is love has also been hurt, let down, disappointed, and heartbroken, but He chooses to love us in spite of these offences. Nowhere else in the Bible is this better demonstrated than in the book of Hosea. In the book of Hosea, God commanded His prophet, Hosea, to go and marry a prostitute named Gomer. Now, God described Gomer as "a woman beloved of her friend . . . an adulteress," which meant that she was an unfaithful woman. God knew that Gomer would not be faithful to Hosea to begin with, which is why He told Hosea to marry her. God wanted Hosea to experience what He was experiencing with the children of Israel. He wanted Hosea to know what it feels like to love someone that rips your heart out of your chest and steps on it. In the book of Hosea 1 verse 2, God said to Hosea, "Go and marry a prostitute, so that some of her children will be conceived in prostitution. This will illustrate how Israel has acted like a prostitute by turning against the LORD and worshiping other gods" (New Living Translation).

God was married to an unfaithful wife, the Nation of Israel, so He wanted his servant, Hosea, to feel what He felt. When Hosea wanted to leave Gomer, God commanded him to love her with "the love of the Lord," the same way He continued to love the Israelites through all of their mess and unfaithfulness.

Gomer was not perfect. She was far from it. Gomer was perfect for Hosea in this case. She was the perfect metaphor for all of mankind in that God loves us but we often refuse to love Him back. And yet, in spite of the way that we treat God, He is still patient, gentle, considerate, respectful of our decisions, understanding towards us, forgiving, and optimistic. So to answer your question, no, you don't have the right to claim that you are too hurt to be as God is and love the seemingly unlovable. You have an obligation as a Believer to love others as God does, especially your spouse. If they hurt you, think about what God did for you. Think about how He forgave you and gave you a chance, after chance, after chance. Think about how God remained faithful as well as optimistic, waiting for the day you would eventually change and come to your senses. Just reflect on how He refused to give up on you even at times you had given up on yourself.

There is a rule we must adhere to when it comes to marriage: The husband is not obligated to earn the respect of his wife no more than the wife is obligated to earn the love of her husband. Love and respect must be given to the spouse regardless of their behavior. Now, that is a hard pill to swallow, but remember, God did not wait for you to earn His love. Instead, He gave it to you although you were undeserving. We must do what is right and follow God's example even if our spouse does not hold up their end of the bargain. When we learn to do things God's way, He will fight on our behalves. Proverbs 16 verse 7 assures us of this when it says, "When a man's ways are pleasing to the LORD, He makes even his enemies to be at peace with him" (New American Standard Bible).

Bouncing back from a marriage freefall begins with one simple principle: No one is perfect. No, not even you because we all have flaws. We all make mistakes. Forgiveness is given when we realize that we are no better than the person we are forgiving, the one that hurt us. If God was willing to forgive us despite of all of the wrong we have done to Him, then we should forgive others in the same manner. In fact, it's a commandment of God to forgive others in the Bible. Forgiveness helps break the cycle of anger, abuse, and revenge, which ravishes so many marriages. That's a start.

The next thing we need to do to turn our marriages around for the good is grow in our relationships with God. My wife and I shock people when we explain to them that our marriage came back from the dead without the help of a marriage counselor. Everyone just assumes that a marriage is doomed without the aid of a marriage counselor, though I am not against counseling. Tiffiny and I turned our marriage around after we both surrendered our lives to Christ. It is a miracle how we stayed together and how we came to this point in our lives. Tiffiny and I filed for a divorce, but while we were in the midst of our divorce, the Army changed the rules for divorce and stated that a soldier cannot get a divorce while they are in a Combat zone. It just so happened that during this time, I was deployed on foreign soil—I was in Iraq. While in Iraq, God preserved me. I was living without purpose. I was suicidal in that I did not have anything to live for. I was empty inside. There was a void inside of me that not even Tiffiny could fill. Finally, I came to a place where I realized that my issues were not the result of anything Tiffiny was or was not doing; they were the result of my lack of a relationship with God. And it was during this time that I surrendered my life to Christ while on leave. The moment I allowed God to take control of my life, I felt a heavy burden lift off me, and I was free from the anger, depression, bitterness, and fear that controlled my life. Before my marriage could change, both Tiffiny and I had to change as individuals. I didn't become a Christian in a church. I did not hear the voice of God while sitting in a beautiful edifice with stain-glassed windows and padded pews. I was in my vehicle driving while intoxicated when the Holy Spirit began to overshadow me. When God's presence entered that vehicle, I instantly sobered up. This supernatural experience taught me that God's power could deliver a person from any addiction, any vice. Not long after God touched my life, He touched Tiffiny's life. She ended up surrendering her life to Christ on her own. During this time, Tiffiny and I had not even talked to each other in over six months, and we were both joyful with our new found love for God and letting the courts handle our divorce. Through what I can only consider being a divine set up, Tiffiny and I ended up having to communicate with each other due to me needing my car transported from Georgia to Colorado. By this point, Tiffiny had given possession of my car to my mother five months before. I needed transportation upon redeployment to the United States, so I contacted everybody that I knew to get this task done for me. Unfortunately, no one could transport my car from Georgia to Colorado. Therefore, I humbled myself and called Tiffiny, who without delay, took time off work and drove my car to Fort Carson, Colorado. During the time she was driving, I communicated with her by telephone periodically to ensure everything went as we discussed, but we did not talk about anything else. God was up to something. And true to form, when I arrived off the plane, Tiffiny had my car there, and she later boarded a plane and headed back to Georgia. When she got back to Georgia, I called her after a few days to say thank you, and we began to talk. Shortly after, the Holy Spirit told me, "Forgive her as I have forgiven you." At that precise moment, I called the lawyer who was handling our divorce, and he said, "Mr. Manuel, I never filed the divorce because I did not think you were serious about getting a divorce." I immediately informed Tiffiny, and she began to tell me how she asked the Lord to come into her life and to give her another chance to be my wife. And today I can attest that God did exactly what Tiffiny asked of him; he preserved us. The only thing we did was learn biblical principles for our lives individually, and our marriage was made whole. It was the year 2005 when God touched our lives and our marriage, and my wife and I have experienced harmony and love, unlike anything we have experienced before. It is simply indescribable.

You can bounce back from a marriage freefall. You can. No marriage is beyond repair. The key to saving your relationship is to change yourself and not your partner. The key to changing yourself is to develop a relationship with God for the sake of living a life that is pleasing in His sight. As Tiffiny and I can testify, God can perform a miracle in your marriage, if you do one simple thing, give yourself to Him!

CHAPTER FIVE

Shaking Off A Ministry Collapse

ONE OF THE MOST NATURAL THINGS IN THE WORLD TO do is to pray. It doesn't take a lot. All you have to do is bow your head, close your eyes, and talk to God who sits above and looks down below. In fact, you don't even have to go through all of those formalities. You can pray with your eyes wide open, while you're driving, while you're working, or while you're in the kitchen cooking. To pray, all you have to do is believe that God is real and that He hears you, and then talk to Him the same way you would your friend or your neighbor. It may seem odd to talk to someone who isn't there physically, but that's where faith steps in. In John 20 verse 29, Jesus told His disciple Thomas, "You believe because you have seen me. Blessed are those who believe without seeing me" (New Living Translation). What impresses God is when you believe in Him and believe His Word without Him having all of the answers in front of you.

Now, praying to God is the easy part; becoming prepared for what you ask for is the more difficult task. I now understand why God does not give us everything we pray for, at least, not right then and there. God knows when we are not prepared for the things we desire of Him. After all, Jesus did tell us to call God "Father" in the Gospels, and a father is someone who is concerned about the well-being of their child physically, mentally, emotionally, and spiritually. Our Father simply wants to ensure that we are asking for the right things and that we are prepared for the things we desire. Sometimes, what we consider to be unanswered prayers are merely God's way of protecting us from our own selfish interests, which may have destructive consequences down the road.

I can attest to the fact that when you are not prepared for the things you want in life, these things will destroy you rather than bless you. Take the time to do your homework before you jump out there and start that business. Take the time to educate yourself before you take on the task of marriage. Take the time to investigate matters before you tackle them. As Jesus said in Luke 14 verse 28, we must "count the cost" before doing anything, including deciding to follow Him. What Jesus was saying is consider the risks and the rewards behind the decision you are about to make. One of the things I did not do when I first entered into pastorship was considering all of the risks associated with such an undertaking. Neither did I consider whether I was truly ready for such a responsibility by seeking counsel from a leader who planted a ministry. Unfortunately, since I did not investigate the process or seek sound counsel, I blindly suffered unnecessary setbacks and defeats in the process. Some of which were minimal costs and others I am still recovering from today. Despite these unforeseen hurdles, mountains, and defeats that I learned in the school of hard knocks, I have learned that if you have been called by the Lord to lead in ministry, you can recover from a ministry collapse. So do not hang your head, throw in the towel, or give up on the vision that God has given you. As the Bible so eloquently declares in Habakkuk 2 verse 3, "For the vision is yet for an appointed time, but at the end, it will speak, and it will not lie. Though it tarries, wait for it; because it will surely come, it will not tarry." The real question here is simple. Do you have the faith and desire to get back up again?

THE PRICE OF BAD IDEAS

In 2 Samuel chapter six, there is the story of King David's successful restoration of the Ark of the Covenant to the capital city of Jerusalem, the City of David. In the year's prior, the Ark of the Covenant (which was a gold-covered wooden chest described in the Book of Exodus as containing the two stone tablets of the Ten Commandments, Aaron, the High Priest's rod, and a jar of manna, which was the bread that God sent down daily from heaven into the Israelites camp while they were living in the wilderness) had been captured by the Israelites' enemies, the Philistines. That day became one of the saddest days in Israelite history. The day the Ark of the Covenant was captured by the Philistines became known as the day the glory of the Lord had departed from Israel (1 Samuel 4:21-22).

Once the Philistines captured the Ark of the Covenant, they paraded it through their towns as a sign of Israel's defeat. They believed that the Ark housed the presence of the Israelite God, Jehovah, not realizing that the Ark was merely a symbol of the presence of God. Interestingly enough was the fact that every town the Philistines carried the Ark into, an epidemic of sickness and disease would break out there. Eventually, the Philistines no longer wanted the Ark of the Covenant around, realizing the danger it posed to them. What had been a blessing to the Israelites had been a curse to the Philistines. So, after seven months of possessing the Ark and suffering as a result of having it around, the Philistines took the Ark of the Covenant and sent it back into Israelite territory on a new cart pulled by two oxen. At first, the Israelites housed the Ark in the Israelite city of Beth-Shemesh, but they later transferred it to the city of Kiriath Jearim (also known as Baalah), a town that was about nine miles west of Jerusalem. There, it was stored in the house of a man named Abinadab and looked after by his son, Eleazar. It was there that King David, being accompanied by over 30,000 elite soldiers in the Israeli military, recovered the Ark of the Covenant.

What should have been the most significant day in the life of King David turned out to be disastrous. Something went wrong that day. David, in his desire and eagerness to recover the Ark, did not take the time to educate himself on the proper procedure for handling the Ark. Apparently, King David did not read the instructions for handling the Ark found in the Torah (the books of the Law written by Moses). David's lack of preparation and his carelessness over handling the Ark resulted in the death of one of his men, Uzzah (2 Samuel 6:6-7, New American Standard Bible). That day, a celebration turned into a funeral; David's laughter turned to mourning, and his joy was eclipsed by the dark cloud of shame and humiliation.

Soon after that startling incident, David became afraid

to house the Ark of the Covenant anywhere close to him, fearing that God would attack him and carry out His wrath on him also. Amazingly, everyone was now afraid of the Ark. David was afraid of it. The Philistines did not want to have anything to do with it. No one wanted to touch it or get anywhere close to it. So, David ordered the Ark to be housed at the nearby home of a man named Obed-Edom, who was a Levite, until he could figure out what to do with it. So the Ark of the Covenant then sat at Obed-Edom's house for the next three months. But amazingly, while the Ark was at Obed-Edom's house, Obed-Edom's household began to experience extraordinary blessings over that course of time like never before. At that point, David realized that there was nothing wrong with the Ark itself; there was, however, something wrong with the way he was handling the Ark. At that point, David began to do the wise thing and research the Ark in the Torah to see how it was to be managed. While reading Moses' instructions on the proper way to handle the Ark, David came across this key verse in Deuteronomy 10 verse 8. "At that time, the LORD set apart the tribe of Levi to carry the Ark of the LORD's Covenant, and to stand before the LORD as his ministers, and to pronounce blessings in his name. These are their duties to this day" (New Living Translation).

Where David had gone wrong was in assigning the wrong people to transport the Ark. Only the Levites were given the task of handling the Ark of the Covenant by God. No one else was allowed to touch or handle it. In essence, only specific hands were consecrated for the task of handling the Ark. Everyone's hands are not ordained to handle holy things, just like everyone is not cut out to perform every work and mission in life. We all have different tasks to accomplish in life, diverse talents and abilities, various passions and callings that were assigned to us before the beginning of time itself. When we try to do that which is assigned to someone else to do in life, we find ourselves failing miserably.

David initially started the journey of returning the Ark of the Covenant to Jerusalem relying on his ideas. He thought that he could do things his way. The truth to success in any venture is not based on our ideas and methods of doing things, but God's predestined assignment for you and His Holy directions to accomplish it. There are procedures and protocol to be followed in everything. There is a way of doing business that guarantees success. There is a way of handling customers that assures more customers. There is a way of marketing that guarantees the right attention and the right customers. There is a way of doing ministry that guarantees success. The most important thing anyone can do to secure their future is to seek knowledge and understanding according to God's will, his way, and his word. Secondly, they need to be abreast of the policies, procedures, systems, and protocols with their desired sphere in life. So learn to exercise patience, consult the Father, become a good listener, and take the time to familiarize yourself with the way things work first, before jumping into anything. Because there is one thing that experience has taught me; you may have good intentions, but if you do anything without consulting the Father and doing your homework, you will more often than not, reap disastrous results.

A HARD PILL TO SWALLOW

Like King David, I entered the ministry not knowing how

things were supposed to work. Rather than seek Godly counsel, I started the ministry with only a heart for God, vision, and passion for people. Based off everything I had ever known, I thought I had everything that I needed to be successful in ministry and shake up the world for Jesus. To couple with those essentials, I had some grand ideas; especially when it came to giving what I considered the have-nots, an opportunity to be leaders in the church. In other words, I believed that most churches overlooked ordinary folk like I grew up with, and would only utilize educated or well-spoken people in positions of authority. So in my eagerness, I was determined at all cost to correct this tragedy in the church. So quite naturally, everyone looking for a position came to our church. But in my youthful exuberance, I lacked wisdom and neglected the Holy Spirit's warning signs in the area of discernment. I thought this would be a simple process: love the people, preach good, sow into their lives, increase members, build bigger, give to the community . . . go on and become great in the Kingdom. I failed to realize that leading a ministry entailed so much more than I had anticipated.

When I started The Kingdom Church, I knew with certainty that I heard from God, and everything was flowing smoothly. The church was growing. In less than a year, the membership had increased to over one hundred people. Now, this might not seem big to some, but if you imagine my wife and I moving halfway across the United States to a city where we did not know one person, this was a phenomenal growth, considering the odds. The word was getting out all over Colorado Springs and Denver about our church. But just as the church was hitting its stride and coming into its own, there was a storm brewing in the distance. And not just any storm, this was a silent one, and it did not come with any warning signs of being dangerous. Furthermore, I did not see this storm beginning because my ambitions blinded me. Like a wildfire that started with the strike of a single match, it took root, and before I knew it, the whole church was on fire. Right under my nose, I naively allowed one undercover member, whom I sought as a leader in the church, to play with matches around our most infant members. To make matters worse, rather than pulling out my fire extinguisher of authority when I smelled the smoke in her presence, I believed that the presence of God would do the hard work for me. But I failed to realize an important key, by placing her in leadership without consulting the Lord she was in essence my problem and not His. As I mentioned earlier, I was determined to appoint "ordinary people" in positions of authority within the church. Since this was my will, I forgot I was responsible for footing the bill. As you can imagine, I was in deep over my head. By waiting for God to handle what I was supposed to handle, I allowed this person's efforts to change things, to throw my wife and me off our game, and to place me in a state of weariness. I was so distracted by the sight of her that ministering on Sundays became difficult because I used all of my energy fighting with her in the spirit. And because I was agitated from her deceptive antics, plots, and silent destruction, all it took was one thing to go wrong to turn everything upside-down and cause pandemonium to erupt in the once-booming church. For the first time, I was able to visualize that portion of Scripture where it says, "a little leaven leavens the whole lump." When you look at this analogy, it also allows one to see how a little leaven is akin to a single cancer cell in the human body. Though the cancerous cell is microscopic, it can destroy the entire body. Like the tiny cell, the bad attitude, backbiting, and underhanded seeds of this one person contaminated our church and began to damage some major organs in the process. As the angel of the house and attending physician, I should have been sued for malpractice for breaking several critical rules in ministry because of this negligent oversight. By the time I regained my composer and dealt with the problem, the emotional damage that she caused was catastrophic, and our most loyal members knew that I failed to protect the flock from the wolf masquerading in sheep's clothing. As a result of my terrible leadership appointment and mishandling the problem, the ministry dwindled in size as people sensing the in-house drama could no longer take it, and I ended up losing the fire and passion that gave The Kingdom Church its purpose. And if I could be honest, this heartache was the avenue that the enemy used to cause me to question my calling and almost caused me to throw in the towel on pastoring.

Though I pray you never experience a ministry collapse like the one I encountered, know that the enemy will attack your ministry at some point if you're winning lost souls for the Kingdom of God. To ensure that you are victorious in the battle over your ministry, I have listed some key rules of ministry that I neglected to keep during my battle, which I listed below:

Rule 1: Do not select leaders for yourself: Ministry does not work like the marketplace, and its leaders are not selected the same as Fortune 500 Companies. God is the only one who determines the leadership within the Body of Christ. If you use resumes, appearances, or preconceived notions to select leaders in the household of faith, more times than not, you will cause yourself and those whom you love, a lot of unnecessary pain. To reinforce this point, we will look at the roadmap known as the Bible. In 1 Samuel, we see how our thoughts, ideas, and eyes can get us into massive amounts of trouble. For here, we look at the children of Israel do the unthinkable; they want to be like all of the other nations, so they desired a king. Now mind you, God was their King, and the results they received with Him were unparalleled by any other nation. He fed them manna from Heaven. God gave them water from a rock. He made the Red Sea part so they could walk on dry ground. He fought and defeated all of their enemies, and above anything else, He loved them unconditionally. With a King like God, why in the world would they desire a king like everybody else? When we look at the Israelites selection of Saul, we find that he looked the part because he was tall, masculine, and a good-looking man, but he lacked one thing that can only come from God, "The Spirit." And without the Holy Spirit, none of us can do anything in the Body of Christ. According to 1 Samuel 15, God told Prophet Samuel, "Saul went to Carmel, and indeed, he set up a monument for himself," and that is exactly what people who are not called by God will do; build monuments for themselves versus obeying God's command. The sad thing is, like Saul and the young lady whom I appointed; these undercover satanic agents give the perception that their motivation is to please God and his people, while their sole mission is to fight against the anointed of God. To ensure that your hands remain clean in the process, I would suggest that you allow the Word of God to prove itself in your ministry, by inquiring God and patiently waiting for Him to send the leader you need. For Jeremiah 3 verse 15 puts it this way, "I will give you shepherds according to my heart, which shall feed you with knowledge and understanding." The hard part for you and I is simple, waiting, but the blessing of obedience will get you, David. Though God's selection may not have been perfect, there is one thing that no one can dismiss. King David was a man after God's own heart, and these are precisely the type of leaders that you need in position in your ministry if you want to experience the Glory of God!

Rule 2: Never fight with God's people: I know this may sound crazy, but fighting those who are fighting you will only work against you in the end. Like it or not, the people in the church still belong to God. You may not like them, but God still loves them and has a plan for them. Take a note from the Prophet Samuel's life who had to overcome his bitterness towards the Israelites when they began to ask God for a king rather than sticking with the theocratic form of government God initially set up for them. Samuel had to repent of his bitterness and go back and start praying for the people again, lest he "sins against God by neglecting to pray" for them (1 Samuel 12:23, King James Version).

Moses is another example of what happens when leaders allow themselves to be drawn into a fight with the sheep they have been assigned by God to lead. Moses lost his temper one day because of the people's constant bickering and complaining, and out of anger, Moses disobeyed God's instruction. God told Moses to speak to the rock, and the water will begin to pour out of it; instead, an angry Moses struck the rock with his rod. Although God still performed the miracle of causing water to flow from a rock, God was upset with Moses' refusal to follow His specific instructions, and therefore, God prohibited Moses from entering into the Promised Land as punishment. In my case, I allowed my frustration with one person to cause me to operate in anger, seclusion, and almost throw in the towel on my God given purpose.

What should you do when the people in your ministry are fighting you? Go to God in prayer and place the situation in His hands. God told us to put our problems in His hands because He wants to fight our battles (Exodus 14:14, King James Version). God told us in Romans chapter twelve to avoid seeking revenge against those who wrong us; but rather, bring our case before Him, and He will avenge us. It's not our job to fight God's people; it's our job to pray for them and let God handle them His way.

Rule 3: Never lose sight of what God called you to do: It can be tempting to stop focusing on your mission and start listening to all the hype and fan fair. Unfortunately, these temptations can cost you to lose your way and put you on a rollercoaster ride to nowhere. Yes, you will experience highs by preaching everywhere and for everybody, but you can lose your ministry while helping others grow theirs. Remember, a pastor is called to shepherd the sheep that God has assigned to your hand. So keep your mind focused on your calling and execute it to the fullest. If you are a pastor, preach the Gospel to your congregants like there is no tomorrow, and live a life that serves as an example of holiness. When pastors do as God instructed and preach His Word with clarity and precision, the hearts and minds of the hearers will be convicted of sin and compelled to accept the Savior, Jesus the Christ. For in that instance, you will be able to experience God's multiplication as the sheep become whole and reproduction takes place, and walls are knocked down so that expansion can take place.

Rule 4: Never forget who called you: Never forget that it is God who called you into the ministry, and not the people. With this in mind, remember that it is God who you will ultimately have to answer to in the end and not the people. Do all that you do to please God, knowing that from Him, you will receive your reward. The people may not like what God is telling you to do, but they are not the boss; God is. Remember, the Bible explains to us who are leaders and teachers of God's Word in James 3 verse 1, "Dear brothers and sisters, not many of you should become teachers in the church, for we who teach will be judged more strictly" (New Living Translation). This means we must keep our focus on feeding God's sheep the truth and avoid succumbing to the temptation to be people pleasers...lest the people perish and their blood end up on our hands and God judge us for it. As leaders over God's people, we have a vital job to perform, one that determines the destination of the souls of men. If we forget that we are working for God to win souls as opposed to working to gain popularity, then we not only fail God, we jeopardize those whom we are called to lead.

I prayed for wisdom, but I delayed in exercising it. I lost sight that ministry was much more than giving people an opportunity to serve, but it also entailed holding people accountable for their actions in the process. I also learned that ministry involved prayer, fasting, and visitations; but it had a business side that leaders cannot afford to neglect. Unknown to those whom you lead, the building comes with a mortgage, utilities come with a utility bill, and conferences have budgets that must be met. While preaching the Word of God and learning to deal with people is always a minister's primary objective in ministry. Those who desire to pastor must understand that pastoring entails more than what appears under the lights, behind the music, and is higher than the fan fair of a good sermon on Sunday morning. Pastoring requires above all things, an undeniable call from God!

THE NEXT TIME

Like King David, I was granted a second chance. I learned from my mistakes. I am glad I made the mistakes that I did so that I could gain the wisdom to not only avoid them, but help other pastors prevent them as well. I had to let go of the shame and embarrassment that I felt as a result of seeing The Kingdom Church dwindle in size—of letting things spiral out of control until I almost walked away from pastoral ministry. I had to extend to myself the same forgiveness I had to extend to that person whom I so negligently allowed to poison the minds of the congregants in our church. By forgiving myself for my mistakes, I emerged from the pit of defeat and fear and got back on my mission. After surviving that assignment, I became a much wiser, experienced, stronger, and humble leader. The culmination of my ministry hardships and those added qualities served as the springboard for me to be elevated to the high office of bishop in the Lord's Church. One thing is for sure, though it was a painful time in my life and ministry, without that terrifying experience, I would probably not have developed into the leader that God has ordained me to become.

If you have ever hit a brick wall in ministry, in business, life, or school, don't wallow in pity, defeat, or allow the enemy to steal your purpose, dream, and vision. Get up, shake yourself off, repent, and get back in the face of God. Remember, you were made for this, and God has not changed his mind concerning you. I can promise you that. If you look close enough, God has already opened a door that no man can close for you to see the vision manifest. So do not be afraid or delay another day, because I am living proof you can get back up from a ministry collapse. Since God is no respecter of persons, if he did it for me, I know he can do it for you!

Get Back Up

CHAPTER SIX

Rebounding From A Sickness

As the writer of the Gospel of John noted, had all of the miracles of Jesus were recorded, there would not be enough books to contain them all. There would be volumes upon volumes of books containing just His miracles alone, not including His many teachings. That is a sea of documented miracles. The miracles of Christ are not only recorded in the Bible; you can find reference to them in the writings of other ancient historians like Flavius Josephus, who spoke of Jesus as having performed many "astonishing deeds."

In what can quickly be referred to as the miracle chapter of the Gospel of Matthew, we see Jesus in action, performing miracles back to back. In Matthew chapter 8, Jesus is going from place to place, healing the sick. The chapter begins with Him descending from a mountain in typical fashion, now ready to be about His Father's business. In the valley below is a multitude of hurting, afflicted, oppressed, bound, and desperate people just waiting for healing, relief, hope, and deliverance. This is the mission field. This is the work. As Christians, let this be the reminder that we need daily to let us know that at some point we must descend from the mountaintops of our religious experiences. Where we enjoy basking in the euphoria of God's divine presence and venture into the valley of the hurting to bring the glad tidings of joy, peace, healing, deliverance, and salvation to those who do not know Christ. We ascend into God's presence to be revived, to get recharged and refueled; but after this, it's back to the valley to do the work of ministry.

After Jesus descended from the mountaintop, He hit the ground running full-speed ahead, being confronted with issue after issue. He met a man with leprosy, a disease that affects the skin, mucous membranes and nerves, and causes discoloration and lumps on the skin; and in severe cases, disfigurement and deformities occur in those affected. Lepers had more to worry about than just the sickness in Jesus' day, and they had to deal with being branded as social outcasts that were forbidden to intermingle with the rest of the population. Lepers had to contend with loneliness and isolation, alongside humiliation and shame. Jesus, not afraid to touch the unclean, extended His hand, touched the man, and declared healing over his body, at which moment, the man was healed. Immediately after that, Jesus was summoned by another person in need of a miracle. While en route to that person's house, He was approached by a Roman centurion whose servant was in dire need of healing. While Jesus was preparing to veer off the path He initially set out on just to go to centurion's house, He was awestruck by the astounding faith of the centurion who expressed his faith in the Savior's ability to heal through words alone. Jesus declared healing over the centurion's servant, praised the man's faith, and continued on His way, healing more people. We see Jesus, throughout the rest of this chapter, healing multitudes of sick and afflicted people and casting out devils, among other miracles. But tucked beneath the many miracles recorded in this chapter is a little incident that rarely gets discussed in the pulpits of churches today, it's the healing of Peter's mother-in-law. Maybe this miracle is not as impressive as walking on water or getting rid of leprosy, but it is a miracle, nonetheless, and one that carries a profound message.

HELP, SERVANT DOWN!

"And when Jesus was come into Peter's house, he saw his wife's mother laid, and sick of a fever. And he touched her hand, and the fever left her: and she arose, and ministered unto them."—Matthew 8:14-15 (New Living Translation)

She was bedridden; unable to get up and do the things she loved doing. Not much is written about Peter's mother-in-law besides what has been recorded above, but from those few words, we get a lot of information about the type of woman she was. The text says Peter's mother-in-law, after receiving her healing, immediately began to "minister to them" ("them" referring to Jesus and the disciples). This woman was a worker; she was a giver; she was a servant at heart. These kinds of people add value to the Body of Christ. These types of workers bring so much joy to the lives of others by helping to relieve us of heavy burdens and bring our dreams and plans to fruition. You do not have to be unique to be a servant; you just need to have the right attitude and perspective in life.

Being a servant means to put others before oneself. As servants, we understand the way the kingdom works; if you bless others, blessings will return to you. If you help make someone else's dream a reality, God will commission someone to make yours a reality. This is called the Law of Reciprocity. Put another way, Jesus said in Matthew 7 verse 12, "Do unto others as you will have them do unto you." Jesus also explained to us in Luke 16 verse 12 that if we can't be "faithful in that which is another man's," then we'll never be trusted with our "own." In essence, what He was saying is we need to learn the value of serving others before we try to lead others. We need to learn how to support other people's visions and goals before we expect other people to support our visions and goals. To receive, you must give; and yet, before you can give, you must first receive. Giving and receiving means we are in a cycle of continually giving and receiving, sowing and reaping. That's the way the Kingdom of God operates, seedtime and harvest time. Sadly, people in the world work this principle more often than Believers. Servants understand their place in the overall scope of things, realizing they're just a small part of the overall picture, rather than seeing themselves as the whole picture.

In Matthew 23 verses 11 & 12, Jesus claimed that between the servant and the one being served, the greater of the two is the servant. He said it this way, "The greatest among you shall be your servant. For whoever exalts himself will be humbled, and whoever humbles himself will be exalted."

Quite often, Jesus found Himself stepping in to settle disputes among His disciples who would often argue among themselves who would be the greatest among them next to Jesus. These men had the wrong perspective and the wrong attitude. They believed greatness was determined by how much praise they received by men and by how big they were in their eyes and the eyes of others. But Jesus tried earnestly to get these men to understand that glorifying oneself is not a sign of greatness. Instead, self-glorification is a sign of pride, which leads to destruction. According to Scripture, Lucifer (now Satan) was destroyed because of his ego, because of his desire to exalt himself above God. Lucifer's famous last words before he lost his position in God's Kingdom and ended up becoming the lord of darkness are deplorable at best. The Book of Isaiah shares with us how crazy this was; "'How art thou fallen from heaven, O Lucifer, son of the morning! How art thou cut down to the ground, which didst weaken the nations! For thou hast said in thine heart, I will ascend into heaven, I will exalt my throne above the stars of God; I will sit also upon the mount of the congregation, in the sides of the north: I will ascend above the heights of the clouds; I will be like the Most High" (King James Version).

As you can see, Lucifer carried a selfish, self-centered, narcissistic, egotistical, conceited, arrogant, and proud attitude. The only person Lucifer was concerned with exalting was himself. He disregarded God's authority and sought to do what he wanted. He did not want to submit to God's order. Instead, he tried to create his own order. He was a rule breaker, a rebel, a heartless individual who would use others to do his bidding. These characteristics describe those who seek to exalt and glorify themselves. Jesus was trying to protect His disciples from falling into this trap, the same trap Lucifer fell prey too. Pride is a trap; it makes us abusive with power, devious, cruel, and causes us to lose the favor and presence of God in our lives.

If Jesus promised that God would exalt those who choose not to exalt themselves but choose to humble themselves instead, then it is important for us to learn how to be humble. The word "humility" is defined as a modest or low view of one's own importance and humbleness." Based on this definition, many people in our society today are filled with pride, which is the absolute opposite of humility. Many people desire to have an inflated view of themselves, and they want to be perceived by others as important, too important to serve others. We train children to be narcissistic in society in an attempt to boost their self-esteem. We train them to focus solely on themselves, on what they want, on how they feel, and often make them think that criticism tossed at them is just some "haters'" attempt to block them in life. We do this in church, too. As pastors, we often make members feel as if whenever things do not work out for them, it's always someone else's fault (namely, the devil's fault). And whenever others reject them, we indicate that it's because the ones rejecting them are "jealous haters," who are intimidated or afraid of them, or people being used by Satan to try to block them. We hardly explain to people in the church that sometimes their thoughts, dreams, and aspirations are rejected because of their own bad attitudes. We have to let certain members know that the reason they cannot keep their jobs is that they do not want to work and follow instructions; not because "the devil does not want to see you blessed." If you have been fired from five jobs in the last thirty days, then that's not a demonic attack against you - the problem is you. If your marriage is in trouble, it's not because Satan is trying to steal your spouse. More than likely, it's because you don't know how to communicate properly and you are not meeting the needs of your spouse. Even Solomon declared in the book of Ecclesiastes that we should avoid being "overly righteous." Which means we sensuously attribute every little occurrence to a spirit, angel, or the devil. Some things we bring upon ourselves, and we must learn the importance of acting responsibly, rather than deflecting blame and responsibility onto others. Likewise, we should train our children to be considerate of others, always considering how their actions affect other people versus themselves. We must teach our children that life is not about them; it's about God and His will for our lives. Rather than looking within for guidance, we must learn to look to God and His Word. The Apostle Paul tells us in Philippians 3 verse 3, "not to put any confidence in the flesh." Jeremiah takes it a step farther when he declares to us the danger of trusting in the flesh and relying on our own hearts, which are "deceitfully wicked."

Jesus urged us to have a low or modest opinion of ourselves. Paul urged us not to "think more highly" of ourselves than we should, but have a sober attitude and perspective of ourselves in Romans 12 verse 3. We should not view ourselves as being more important than others. We should not allow our money and titles to cause us to have an exaggerated view of ourselves. We may all be uniquely designed by God, but we're not irreplaceable. There is always someone who can do what you do, perhaps even better than us. When we have been blessed by God to be in a position of authority and influence, then we should not look at ourselves as if we are so good or great that we deserve to be where we are. Sure, we may have worked hard to get to certain places in life, but God is the one who deserves the glory. If not for life, health and strength, the use of our limbs, and the many other miracles that we take for granted, we would have been swallowed up whole by sin and death.

In Daniel chapter 4, there was a man who was pumped up with pride and viewed himself with an exaggerated view, and his name was Nebuchadnezzar, king of Babylon. Nebuchadnezzar thought he was a living god. He ordered that a ninety-foot golden statue of himself be erected so that the citizens of his kingdom could worship him. Every citizen had been ordered to bow down and worship this golden image. Due to Nebuchadnezzar's arrogance towards God, God humbled him by causing him to lose his mind and wander around on the outside of the walls of the kingdom like a beast, eating grass while crawling on all fours. The king's mental state was impaired for seven years. After God decided that the king had enough, He restored his mind and let him resume his role as king of Babylon. Assuredly, Nebuchadnezzar never viewed himself as a god again. He was just glad to be considered a human again. We should take the king's experience literally and use it as a template to keep us grounded because we do not want to force God to remind us who is in charge. Trust me; we would not like him humbling us like he did Nebuchadnezzar.

The Bible tells us in Proverbs 16 verse 18 that pride goes before destruction. God hates a "proud look." Likewise, in Proverbs 6 verse 17, God expresses how he hates pride because it embodies the very attitude of Satan. So when a person thinks they are too big and too important to serve, God becomes disgusted with them for opposing Him. On the opposite side of pride is humility, which attracts God to us and compels Him to bless us. Humility attracts God, which also suggests that humility attracts God's blessings and presence, which contains healing and delivering power. This is what is so significant about the passage of Scripture dealing with Peter's mother-in-law because it reveals the type of attitude this woman possessed. An attitude that made her a top priority of Jesus', even in the midst of His incredibly demanding schedule.

GOD IS A HEALER

During my time as pastor of The Kingdom Church, I experienced a day that I will never forget. Tired from the hustle and bustle of ministry, I began to notice that I had a cold that seemed to be getting the best of me. Despite taking over the counter medications for two weeks, rather than getting better, my condition seemed to get worse. Now any preacher can tell you, crafting a sermon is hard work even in an ideal situation. So one could only imagine how difficult it could be to craft a message after you have been sick for two weeks. Oh, by the way, I was responsible for delivering a message every Wednesday night, Friday night, and two sermons on Sunday morning. So if you have done the math, that is four messages per week. But pastors do not get the luxury of calling in sick or taking extensive time off. Sick or not, pastors have to be available to those whom they serve, and anybody will tell you, if a pastor is outside of the pulpit for more than a week, parishioners will either stay home or attend another church. In my case, the ministry was only a year old, so I did not have anybody who could manage this responsibility. Like pastors around the world, I roughed it out until things got so rough that my wife had to rush me to the emergency room. And let me tell you, I was not prepared for the news I was about to receive. At worst case, I suspected that I had a bad cold, the flu, or at worst, pneumonia.

To my surprise, my examination revealed something worse. I had blood clots in my lungs, and the doctor said I arrived at the hospital just in time. Her exact words to my wife and me were as such; "Sir, you are in critical condition." And what she said next floored me, "if we delay in treatment, you will die."

All of us could die at any time, but presently, I was only thirty-five years old, and death was not something I was ready to face. To double-check her diagnosis, the doctor ordered X-rays and an ultrasound. Just as she had suspected, I had blood clots in my lungs, and if one reached my heart, Tiffiny would have to decide which funeral home to prepare my body for burial and what day to have my funeral. Now I realized this was not a dream when the social worker was called in to talk to us before I was admitted. She asked questions like; do you have a living will? Do you consider your wife as your next of kin? At that moment, it was if I was frozen in time, and all I remember saying to God is that I trust you. The next thing I remember is the nurse telling us after the first injection that Tiffiny could not stay in the room with me. So we prayed the prayer of faith, and I looked her in the eyes and told her to go home and prepare for service tomorrow. Surprisingly, I was not afraid of what could happen, but I did ask God if it was His will for me to die at this time. True to form, the Word of God proved to be true. When I asked God, He answered me in His still small voice; you will not die. From that moment I decided to trust God and not the X-rays, ultrasound, or the doctor's diagnosis. Instead, I remembered what Jesus told Jairus, "Despite everyone else's opinion, only believe." So I did something that I had not done since I was sick, I went to sleep, and sure enough, I opened my eyes to the dawn of a new day. And that is what you have to do, despite the tests and the doctor's medical opinion, believe the Lord. This experience taught me that God is a healer and He watches over His Word. To show you how amazing God is, after performing a test the next morning, the doctor stopped the medication, gave me discharge papers, and told me they must have made a mistake in their diagnosis because they did see any signs of blood clots in my body. From that moment on, I began laying hands on the sick in faith and believing God to do what He had done for me and Peter's mother-in-law - a miracle. And because of the grace and mercy that God has given to me, I am determined to serve in the Kingdom of God until He calls me to eternal rest. As for you, it is time to stop feeling sorry for yourself, pick up your Bible, and declare the Word of God over your life. One thing is for sure, your best days are ahead of you, and you can get back up from a sickness.

THE SIN-SICKNESS CONNECTION

There is a connection in the Bible between sin and sickness. For starters, Genesis chapter three indicates that sickness entered the earth as a result of the curse caused by Adam's act of disobedience. Secondly, certain emotions which God warns us about, such as unforgiveness and bitterness are causes of sicknesses as revealed by researchers. So when God tells us to forgive others and release resentment out of our hearts, He's not only trying to preserve our spirits, but our bodies as well. Still, there is another sin-sickness connection to explore. James 5 verses 13 - 16 says, "Is anyone among you suffering? Then he must pray. Is anyone cheerful? He is to sing praises. Is anyone among you sick? Then he must call for the elders of the church, and they are to pray over him, anointing him with oil in the name of the Lord, and the prayer offered in faith will restore the one who is sick, and the Lord will raise him up, and if he has committed sins, they will be forgiven him. Therefore, confess your sins to one another, and pray for one another so that you may be healed. The effective prayer of a righteous man can accomplish much" (New American Standard Bible).

Notice the language utilized within the Text. James connects physical illness with unconfessed sin and impenitence by explaining that restoration to God brings not just physical healing but also forgiveness of sins. On the flip side of this, the absence of restoration in Christ allows sickness to continue and sins to go unforgiven. Furthermore, in 1 Corinthians 11 verses 27 - 30, we find these words: "Therefore, whoever eats the bread or drinks the cup of the Lord in an unworthy manner shall be guilty of the body and the blood of the Lord. But a man must examine himself, and in so doing he is to eat of the bread and drink of the cup. For he who eats and drinks, eats and drinks judgment to himself if he does not judge the body rightly. For this reason, many among you are weak and sick, and a number sleep (meaning "dead")" (New American Standard Bible).

Paul also stated that there was a connection between sin and sickness when he revealed that those who take communion unworthily, which means to disregard the literal meaning of the bread and wine of the communion which symbolizes flesh and blood of Jesus. More importantly, Holy Communion symbolizes our relationship with Christ. To profane the communion by taking it as an expression of your allegiance to Christ when you have not surrendered your life to Christ is to lie about having a relationship with God when you don't have one. According to Romans 8 verse 1, "it is for this reason that sicknesses come upon some, and to remain outside of Christ is to continue to live in sin."

Lastly, according to Luke 13 verse 11, we find a reference made by Jesus to a "spirit of infirmity" that had afflicted a woman for eighteen years. What this suggests is that demonic spirits cause some sicknesses. We invite demons into our lives through sin and disobedience towards God. The connection here is this: Whenever we operate in rebellion towards God, we open up the door in our lives for spirits to bring all kinds of sicknesses and diseases upon us, both physically and mentally, as was the case with King Saul in 1 Samuel 16 verse 14 and King Nebuchadnezzar in Daniel chapter 4. In Matthew 7 verse 15, it is revealed to us that a young boy's seizures and lunacy were the results of a demon spirit. The same goes for the demoniac in Mark chapter 5. In both cases, psychological illnesses came about as a result of demonic possession.

Now, I'm not saying that every sickness we experience is a result of sin and demonic spirits. The body is bound to experience sickness at some point. Just because you caught a cold, don't start rebuking Satan. Just because your toe hurts, don't go and blame a demon. Some sicknesses are simply a result of bad eating habits, stress, and age. However, using wisdom, we cannot rule out all of the potential sources of an affliction. We need to take the practical and the spiritual approach and eliminate factors until we pinpoint the exact source.

TESTIFY OF GOD'S GOODNESS

Like Peter's mother-in-law, when God heals us from a sickness, we need to jump up and start serving in His Holy Kingdom.

One of the best ways to serve God is to tell others about His healing grace and power. Let those around you know that God is a healer. Go and share the message of salvation with everyone you know.

The reason that God heals and blesses us is not so we can live comfortably, but He does these things, so we have a testimony to share with those who do not know Him. As Paul explained in 2 Corinthians 3 verse 3, "we are God's written epistles." In essence, God set it up where people cannot only discover Him in the Bible, but they can also see Him through our lives. So let your life be an open book, reveal what God has done, and let the world know our God is amazing!

CHAPTER SEVEN

It Was All Just Preparation

THE MOST SIGNIFICANT TEACHER IN LIFE ARE THE experiences one has encountered in life. It's our experiences that teach us how to trust God, make good decisions, and avoid pitfalls. I'm not saying that head knowledge is not necessary. I have several college degrees, and I have learned much from sitting under mentors, but my greatest lessons came as a result of falling and then bouncing back from falls. Experiences took that which I read and heard about and made it personal to me. Now, I don't just tell people God is real; I testify of the realness of God because I've personally seen Him perform miracle after miracle in my life. My passion comes across to others when I'm speaking of the things my wife and I have personally experienced, and to that I say, praise God because my afflictions served a purpose.

Apparently, God Himself believes that life is the best teacher. Throughout His Word, we see numerous examples of God using different experiences to teach humanity lessons. We see in the book of Hosea, God teaching man the power of forgiveness and reconciliation, by commanding His prophet to love a woman who was seemingly unlovable. In the book of Genesis, we see God teaching Abraham a valuable lesson in the area of obedience and sacrifice as He commanded him to take his only son, which he waited so long to have, up Mount Moriah to sacrifice him on an altar. Can you imagine how distraught Abraham must have been? Can you imagine how much of a nervous wreck he was, or how conflicted he had to have been at that moment? I could only imagine the type of thoughts that must have been running through Abraham's mind at that moment. One thing is for sure; he was not happy and excited about following God's instructions, but he did it out of obedience to the Father. Of course, God stopped Abraham before he could deliver the deathblow to his son, Isaac, upon that altar; and even provided Abraham with a ram in the bush as an alternative to his son. But that experience taught Abraham a valuable lesson about obedience and loyalty, and it also shows us today a valuable lesson about the dilemma God Himself had to face when it came to dealing with humanity. God had to sacrifice His Son on the cross just to save us, and there was no substitutionary ram caught in a thicket that could ease His burden and pain. Jesus Himself had to "learn obedience by the things which he suffered," as revealed in Hebrews 5 verse 8. Although Jesus was God in the flesh, He had to endure. Although He was omniscient even as a child; able to school even the most educated intellectuals at the age of twelve while in the Jewish Temple one day, Jesus still had to undergo specific experiences before He could mature and develop into the Savior of the world. Now that's saying something, head knowledge may inform you, but experience prepares you for where God is taking you. Experience serves as preparation to mature you and condition you to endure and persevere over the things you will have to go through to obtain the blessings God promised you. So don't curse your pain, and stop asking God to remove you from the test. Know that through these experiences, God is preparing you to walk in greatest.

One passage of Scripture that always amazes me is the one found in Exodus chapter four. Here we find the story of one of God's most celebrated and recognized prophets, Moses. God wanted to prepare Moses for the journey ahead, so he called him to be the deliverer of His people, the Israelites. He met Moses in the desert, manifesting His presence in the form of a burning bush. While speaking with Moses, God began to demonstrate His power in various ways. He had Moses first throw down his staff. Upon hitting the ground, the staff turned into a serpent. God then instructed Moses to do the one logical thing that common sense tells us not to do: pick the snake up by the tail. God was teaching Moses to trust Him, no matter how crazy His instructions may seem. But the thing that God did next is what baffles me as a lifelong student of ministry; He instructed Moses to stick his hand into his cloak. Moses obeyed, and after he pulled his hand out of his cloak, he noticed that it was leprous. Why did God afflict Moses with a deadly disease at that moment? It was to teach Moses a valuable lesson, not only about the supernatural ability of God to heal, but also to have compassion on those he was getting ready to lead. The people Moses was getting ready to lead would need to be cleansed from the impurities of Egypt, and they would have to be cleansed from the impurity of sin. The Israelites were people who had become filthy over the years, and would need a compassionate leader to lead them, not someone out of touch with the struggles they faced.

If there is one thing your pain and suffering will teach you in life, it is to operate with the spirit of compassion needed to reach the people God has called you to. If you cannot understand their afflictions, you will never be able to speak their language and gain their trust and attention. That's why God allowed you to suffer a fall. That's why God let you experience rock bottom. That's why God let you get hurt, disappointed, stabbed in the back by those you trusted the most. That's why God let your family cast you aside and leave you for dead. That's why God allowed you to go through that season of hardship where it seemed as if Hell was breaking loose and you could not appear to catch a break. God allowed you to experience all those things for the same reason Jesus came to earth to experience what you and I go through. God wanted you to be touchable. As the author of Hebrews explains about Christ: "For we do not have a high priest who cannot sympathize with our weaknesses, but One who has been tempted in all things as we are, yet without sin" (New American Standard Bible).

Jesus not only hears our prayers, but he feels our hearts and understands our pains. Why? So He could prove to you how much He loves you and to show you how to go through the fire and storms of life. He went through the fire and the flood, faced the temptations, experienced the disappointments; and yet, He, through His example, showed us how to endure these things and not get sidetracked. Likewise, realize that there is a reason you are going through the things you are facing right now. Understand that you have a mission ahead of you and your experiences today are preparing you for your God-ordained purpose. God is preparing you to go to people who need you, who need what you have. Your troubles are merely the boot camp God is using to whip you into shape. So stop feeling sorry for yourself and lying on the ground of misery, and get up from that depression. It's time for you to see your situation for what it is. Not a lifestyle, but a training camp.

Do not let anybody fool you, to have a testimony; you must first have a test. God is shaping you into material evidence for others to behold and be inspired by your resilience. Your troubles are not here to destroy you but to be the catalysts that launch you into your destiny. It's time for you to bounce back. How? One simple step, "Consider it all joy, my brethren, when you encounter various trials, knowing that the testing of your faith produces endurance. And let endurance have its perfect result, so that you may be perfect and complete, lacking in nothing" (James 1:2-4, New American Standard Bible).

REJOICE!!! That's right; you read that correctly. Rather than mope and complain about where you are in life, start lifting your hands and thanking God because you are in the perfect spot to be used by the Father. God does not need a perfect vessel, and neither is He interested in a perfect setting. God can go into the crack house and snatch the taste right out of an addict's mouth with His anointing. God will show up in the bedroom in that hotel that serves as a haven for prostitution and cleanse your plans to fornicate. God will meet you in a prison cell and wipe away the tears that are streaming down your face. God can and will show up in the roughest of places to rescue His children and those whom He loves. What good is light if it cannot shine in the darkness? The answer is simple; darkness is what allows light to reveal its purpose.

You are the light that God ordained to shine in your family. You are the salt that God has ordained to add flavor to your ministry, and you are the miracle that the world needs to witness rising from the ashes. So shake yourself off from that ministry collapse. Get back up from that marriage free fall. Free yourself from that financial prison, and declare your healing from that sickness that has been tormenting you. For in your refusal to stay down, you become proof to unbelievers that with God, it is possible to get back up again.

Though I have thoroughly enjoyed this journey with you, we have come to the time and place where you have to close this book and put into action the principles you have learned. Remember, like the ball on the court of life, you cannot advance, be useful to others, or score points for the Kingdom of God without bouncing back in the hands of God over and over and over again.

Let us pray: Father, I thank you for this time and opportunity that you have afforded us to realize your excellent plan for our life. We ask you, Father, to forgive us for the times we have given up on life, and thrown in the towel because of rough experiences. Today, we understand that every hill, mountain, and valley experience was never designed to harm us, but was there to teach us how to be dependent upon you. Cover us with the precious blood of Jesus and empower us with your Holy Spirit, that we may get back up again and become living epistles for you. These things we ask in the name of Jesus, Amen!

REFERENCES

CHAPTER ONE

1. Richard Dawkins, *The God Delusion*, Houghton Mifflin, New York, 2006. pg. 56.
2. Friedrich Wilhelm Nietzsche, *The Antichrist*, 1895.
3. Friedrich Wilhelm Nietzsche, *Thus Spoke Zarathustra*, 1891.
4. Karl Marx, *Introduction to A Contribution to the Critique of Hegel's Philosophy of Right: Collected Works, v. 3*. New York. 1976.

CHAPTER TWO

1. Psychology Today, *Harvard Study Pegs How Parental Substance Abuse Impacts Kids*. (https://www.psychologytoday.com/blog/the-athletes-way/201607/harvard-study-pegs-how-parental-substance-abuse-impacts-kids)
2. Journal of Clinical Child and Adolescent Psychology, *Relation of Positive and Negative Parenting to Children's Depressive Symptoms* (https://www.ncbi.nlm.nih.gov/pmc/articles/PMC3152307/)

ABOUT THE AUTHOR

Dr. Teco L. Manuel is a United States Army Retiree, Disabled American Veteran who was injured during Operation Iraqi Freedom, and duly consecrated Bishop in the Lord's Church. As one dedicated to lifelong learning, Dr. Manuel completed his undergraduate studies at Shorter University, Master of Theology from Omega Bible Institute & Theological Seminary, and Doctor of Ministry from the International College of Ministry. Dr. Manuel was duly consecrated a Bishop in the Lord's Church by the International College of Bishops with a valid line of Apostolic Succession, and he is a member of the illustrious Joint College of Bishops. Though he has been blessed beyond measure, Dr. Manuel's joy and balance in life are his wife, Tiffiny, affectionately known as Lady T, and his son, Tyler.

To contact the author, go to:

DrTecoManuel@gmail.com
Facebook: Teco Lamones Manuel
Twitter: Teco Lamones Manuel
Instagram: Teco Lamones Manuel